SUCCESS REQUIRES ACTION

SUCCESS REQUIRES ACTION

STRATEGIES FOR THE ENTREPRENEURIAL CHALLENGED AUTHOR

NATE FORTNER

Whosoever Press

Whosoever Press books may be ordered through booksellers or by contacting:

Whosoever Press
P.O. Box 1513
Boaz, AL 35957
www.whosoeverpress.com
1-256-706-3315

ISBN-13: 978-0692664711 (SB)
ISBN-13: 978-0-692-67215-0 (HB)

Library of Congress Control Number: 2016904641

Printed in the United States of America

Whosoever Press date: 4/1/2016

Edited by: Christy Smith, Caron Suzanne Davis, Glen Abernathy

You Must Commit to Success!

Dedication

This book is dedicated to every Whosoever Press author. You have believed in me as your Publisher to help get your book out to the world. Some titles are easier than others, no doubt, and I thank you for the challenge. I'm 100% committed to your success, and I personally believe in you! You all have your own ministries and goals for your books, and each title is unique. I pray that you find success as a writer in all of your endeavors.

Entrepreneur

A person who organizes and operates a business or businesses, taking on greater than normal financial risks in order to do so.

You will find that this book contains strategies for the entrepreneurial challenged Author

Winners Don't Quit, They Commit!

How to Build a Successful Empire from Nothing

Contents

Introduction

Chapter 1 How I Cut My Income in Half
and Doubled My Work Load   1

Chapter 2 Defeat Extinction by Growing Your Army
and Equipping your Soldiers with the
Right Weapons   5

Chapter 3 Remembering the Days before Internet Marketing   13

Chapter 4 What is an Author's Platform?   15

Chapter 5 The Dollar is Bouncing Back From Poverty   19

Chapter 6 Why You Need to Market   21

Chapter 7 Determining Your Audience   25

Chapter 8 Your Website   29

Chapter 9 Miscellaneous Low Cost Ideas to Promote Your Book   33

Chapter 10 Cracking the Article Writing Code   39

Chapter 11 Overnight Success as a Writer   41

Chapter 12 Creating Quality Do-It-Yourself Marketing Content   43

Chapter 13 How Can I Make More Money?   49

Chapter 14 A Bad Cover Will Cost You Sales   55

Chapter 15 Adjusting the Price of Your Book   57

Chapter 16 My Take on Network Marketing   59

Chapter 17 Partnership Marketing   61

Chapter 18 Poor is No Excuse   65

Chapter 19 The Authors Pledge of Success   67

Chapter 20 The Broken Trap Called God   69

Chapter 21 Faith is Overrated   71

Chapter 22 The Favor Factor   73

Chapter 23 King David's Five Stones of Business Success   75

Chapter 24 The Making of a #1 Best Seller   81

Chapter 25 Videos Gone Wild (Viral)   83

Chapter 26 Don't Disrespect Your Publisher   85

Chapter 27 Without Faith in Yourself...   89

Chapter 28 No More Prancing Reindeer on our #RedCup   93

Chapter 29 Coffee Sleeve Marketing   95

Chapter 30 Recording Radio Interviews   99

Chapter 31 Top 3 Free Marketing Avenues for Authors   103

Chapter 32 Social Media Marketing   107

Chapter 33 26 Social Media Platforms You Should be Using   109

Chapter 34 How Do I Get an ISBN for My Book?   111

Chapter 35 How Do I Purchase a Library of Congress Number for My Book?   113

Chapter 36 How Can I Turn My Paperback Book Into an Audio Book?   115

Chapter 37 Why All the Crappy Books?   117

Chapter 38 How Can People Subscribe to My Blog on Blogger?   119

Chapter 39 3 Killer Tips to Growing a Successful Business   121

Chapter 40 Congratulations!   127

Chapter 41 Fascinating Pastoral Tactics That Can Help Your Business Grow   129

Chapter 42 Title Generators   131

Chapter 43 Telemarketing Made Easy   133

Chapter 44 Storms in the Night   135

Chapter 45 The Locked Door of Soliciting   137

Chapter 46 The Invisible Streams   139

Chapter 47 You Need a Comprehensive Bookstore Contact List   141

Chapter 48 I Need a Vacation!   141

Chapter 49 Dangerous Marketing   143

Chapter 50 Persistence Isn't Pestering, It's Educating   145

Chapter 51 Jesus Was a Business Man   147

Chapter 52 You Need a Comprehensive List of Libraries   149

Chapter 53 Vision in the Ashes   151

In Closing

Resources for Authors

Catalog

About the Author

Success Isn't Free!

Success Isn't Given!

Success Isn't Even Earned!

It's Made!

Introduction

This is the question I hate hearing from authors, especially mine. *"Why aren't my books selling?"* It kills me, as a creative person, when people don't buy my music or the books I've written. I feel even worse, as a Publisher, when authors I've published can't get their books off the ground. I know from what I've read online, that supposedly, most Publishers leave the marketing and promotion up to the authors themselves. I totally agree that a Publisher can't build an author's platform for them. As a Christian Author, writing about Christian Living topics, I wouldn't want anyone trying to build my platform. They don't know me like I do. They don't know my personal convictions like I do. It would in all honesty be unfair to the author for a Publisher to try and build the author's platform. Only the Author can do that.

However, I feel that I owe it to my Authors to equip them with resources that will help to train them in the direction they should go. Ultimately, it will depend on how much money you have to market and promote your work. It's going to require countless hours of dedication and hard work to get your name, brand and message out there. If you've been following me for any length of time at all, then you know you need money to operate your business. Again, as an author, your book is your business.

As an author though, you need someone guiding and directing you in the right direction. I've never been traditionally published, and I don't know all the In's and

Out's of the Publishing World, but I need to get attention for myself if I want to see money rolling my way.

My Company, WhosoeverPress.com, was established in 2012. My goal was to help writers make their dreams of being published a reality. I know what it's like to have a dream, and most of my life, it's been left up to me to make my dreams come true all on my own. To date, I've published about a dozen authors. Ten authors in three years is pretty good, I think. I've made myself available to them 24/7. They can call me anytime for help or advice, and they all have my personal cell number. Even though I can't force them to get out and hustle, I still want them to be successful. I believe in them! I've been able to get my authors books into distribution to over 35,000 retailers world-wide. I had the privilege of seeing one of my new authors blossom this past weekend in a church service, when she began testifying of God's goodness in her life. She started sharing about how she had been in jail for this and that, but God set her on the path to righteousness. I personally knew this author before I published her book, and I've seen her fight some of her personal battles, even in her health. I couldn't help but tear up when I saw Jeana Willis, author of *"Keep On Walking"* position herself on that stage, and began to proclaim the goodness of God. At that moment, it was almost as if I had heard the voice of God whisper in my ear, *"You helped her discover her purpose!"*

I was recently in the home of Whosoever Press Author, Courtney Kinneman, author of the "Agnes the Awful" series. I have personally seen a transformation in her life and the lives of her children over the past six months. All I can say is, God is doing something incredible in their lives. I saw her tear up as she began talking about her kids and how she wants to feed hungry families for the holidays. I see people like Jeana Willis and Courtney Kinneman, who are passionate about what they do, and I have to re-evaluate my own life. I'm constantly asking myself, "Am I doing all I can possibly do? Could I give a little more in certain areas of my life?"

I've always been taught to never give up. Chase your dreams, reach for the stars, and you can do anything you set your mind to accomplish. In my thirty years of life, I've noticed, one is praised for believing in themselves, except for writers. Writers are repeatedly rejected by the Traditional Publishing Houses for believing in themselves, and they drop into this major depression. I've always been told that my heart is bigger than my wallet. I know what it's like to be rejected in life, and so I have this desire to help others succeed. I even offered to pay for a friend of mine to come to Alabama and record his next music project. The guy ended up blasting me on Facebook a few months later, saying I was wrong about some of my personal beliefs. So, I understand that some people will never appreciate all we do for them, but I can't be mean to people. I love to see people blossom into what God has designed them to do with their lives. I wish I was wealthy enough so I could help more people

I may never understand why good books are rejected by big name Publishing Houses, but one thing's for sure, I will be here to continue encouraging writers to believe in themselves. WhosoeverPress.com will continue to publish writers, and help them to sell their books. We don't promise fame and fortune, but I'll help you any way I can. I've had people help me in the past couple years to get recognized, so I want to pass it along. I've been on national television, nominated for awards for my songs, and even been on numerous radio shows. I've recently even been published and interviewed for magazines. I've accomplished a lot in just three years of starting Whosoever Press, but I'm not satisfied. I will not be satisfied until my authors and I are household names.

I've had my authors do radio interviews at real radio stations, online radio shows, and even on my personal online radio show, The Author Minute. I've even had some of my authors on TV for interviews. It makes me happy to see each of them walking in their calling. It may sound strange, but I feel as though they are like my children, and it makes me, as their Publisher proud of them when they are fulfilling their purpose.

There is an enigma that discredits authors who self-publish their own books. They are looked down on in the literary world as garbage books that will never amount to anything. Don't believe me? Get online and research how to self-publish a book, and you will see multiple negative comments directed toward self-published authors. This is what I don't understand! We constantly encourage people to believe in themselves except for in writing. It almost makes you feel that if a publisher doesn't like your manuscript, then you might as well use it as fuel to roast marshmallows. It's an abomination to the world and shame on you for believing in yourself! Sorry, but I just don't agree with that logic! I know an author who I engage with on a daily basis who started out as a self-published author and is now a New York Times Bestselling Author! Grant Cardone, author of *"The 10X Rule"* self-published a book and became a New York Times Best Selling Author! December of 2014, I discovered Grant Cardone on YouTube while searching for Zig Ziglar videos. In March of 2015, only three months later, I quit my day job of eight years. Within six months of devouring Grant's content, I landed a $12,000.00 book deal and dominated the market. Other Publishing Companies were even offering to match my price, but I got the deal. This was a 750 page hardback book. Once I secured the book deal, I had to figure out how in the world I was going to print a hardback book. We had only been publishing paperback books up to this point. I committed first and figured out the rest later. In 1997, Robert Kiyosaki, author of *"Rich Dad, Poor Dad"* self-published his book and in just an hour episode on the Oprah Show, he sold 1,000,000 copies of his book.

I had a woman call my office last year asking me what type of publisher I considered myself. I knew what she was getting at, so I said, *"I take garbage books and help them to blossom into beautiful pieces of art!"* She started dogging me for giving bad writers hope. She continued on saying that I should be ashamed of myself for encouraging bad writing. *"You're just another Vanity Press!"* she screamed through the phone as she hung up on me. Just to clarify, the word Vanity means empty or worthless. I most certainly do not believe that my writing or that the writing of any of my authors is empty or worthless! I believe in Whosoever Press authors! Royalties are zero to none sometimes, but at other times, royalties run as fresh as the waves on a paradise island.

I don't know all the answers to making books fly off the shelves, but I'm committed to myself and my authors. Within three years, I have written an article for a Hollywood film, hosted a major Movie Premier where a Movie Producer and one of the actors came to our town. I have even been nominated for an award. Pretty cool, if you ask me! Check out: www.BrothersKeeperFilm.com. So if you're one of those writers who don't believe in encouraging others, don't bother submitting your manuscript to my company. We work together to help make a difference in the lives of those we meet. I want my authors to be successful! I don't know what other Publishers are doing for their authors, I just know what I'm doing for mine.

Scan QR Code

Or Type the link below into your web browser
https://www.youtube.com/watch?v=mLLR7gxOV-s

Scan QR Code

Or Type the link below into your web browser
https://www.youtube.com/watch?v=rcQ5vNtkGA4

CHAPTER 1

How I Cut My Income in Half and Doubled My Work Load

One of the greatest decisions I've ever made in growing my business was to create a catalog. In 2015, I started a promotional product line here at WhosoeverPress.com My authors were going elsewhere to buy their business cards, bookmarks, flyers, and other marketing materials. I found this to be a financial loss for my business. I researched and found a way to provide my authors with a one-stop publishing shop. Publishing, marketing, advertising, and distribution all wrapped up and ready in one place.

The only problem with my current business plan is that I don't have a store front location for my company. I run my company from my home. Yes, I'm a legal company and I pay taxes, so don't ask. I do what Uncle Sam requires of me. When I'm not publishing an author, I'm not making money. When I'm not making money, by the end of the month, I may be at your house looking for food. The point is, not enough people know my company exists. Whether you're willing to admit it or not, you have the same problem as me. Obscurity!

That is when I decided I would create and distribute a catalog to promote the services that I provide as a company. First, I made sure all my current business clients received a copy of the catalog. Second, I started at one end of town and worked my way to the other end delivering catalogs to every business I passed. Currently, I'm still printing and distributing catalogs. Many businesses with whom I already had a business relationship were shocked to learn the additional assistance I could provide to help their business growth.

I take at least two hours per day walking into businesses and introduce myself as the owner of WhosoeverPress.com. Before I leave, I give the Owner or Manager a catalog. I also ask them for a business card. When they give me their card, I give them one of mine in return. Many times in the exchange, they are so impressed with the quality of my work that they want to order right away. If they don't recognize the quality that I offer, I make a last minute pitch before walking out of their business.

Three weeks ago, within a few hours, I delivered thirty catalogs around town. Before I even got back to my office to start Cold Calling, I received a call from the Owner of one of the local Ford Dealerships. He was calling me after looking over my catalog wanting to do business with me. This week, I picked up a check from the same car dealership for over $500.00 on just one deal.

Creating this catalog has probably been the most beneficial key to growing my company. The point is, I'm working on getting out of obscurity. I quit my job of eight years in March of 2015. Quitting my job was stupid for many reasons, but it possibly saved my life. I may tell you that story later, but in my opinion, you shouldn't quit your day job until your business is at least covering your monthly bills. When I quit my job, I was grossing about $30,000.00 per year. Now, I'm grossing about $15,000.00 to $20,000.00. I took a major pay cut, so I had to cut my monthly bills from around $1,200.00 per month down to around $500.00 per month. I'm living way below my means. With this said, why would you continue to read the rest of this book knowing I'm not loaded? The answer is simple. If I don't work, I seriously won't be able to eat and pay my bills. I'm single and I don't have a wife and kids, so it's just me. I wouldn't advise anyone with a family to just up and quit their job without banking some serious cash first.

The reason this book is going to change your life is because it's life changing material. The content in this book is the real deal things I've done. I've made on my own at least half the income I was making working the 9 to 5. Obviously, I'm doing something right. I'm not where I want to be, but I'm going in the right direction. Now instead of working 8 to 10 hour shifts every day, I work 16 hours per day. When I quit my job, I had enough money in the bank to last me six months. So, in other words, I had six months to make it or break it! Did I take a vacation? Nope! I worked my butt off! Am I rich? Nope! Do I live pay check to pay check? Nope. How do I survive? I work my butt off every single day pushing and pulling to get people to know who I am. Some weeks, I make killer profit, while other weeks, I scrape to get by.

Why are you still reading this book? I'll tell you exactly why. I'm still making 75% of the income I was making working a dead end job. Who else do you know that has ever up and quit their job, and was still capable of producing 75% of their income on their own the very next year? Before you quit your job, you better make sure you have some cash in the bank. Depending on where you live, you will have to figure out how much money you need to live on. You need money in the bank to cover the slow months. Trust me, there will be massively slow months around the holidays if you're not prepared. I took a very hard hit the last quarter of 2015. This is just me personally, but I'm not a big spender either. You may need $50,000.00 to $100,000.00 in the bank before you can quit your job. Again, it really depends on the cost of living where you live. What are my profit projections for next year? I'll keep you guessing.

The point of this chapter is not to brag about how I cut my income in half and doubled my work load. That business model sounds completely stupid! This chapter is to show you that you can achieve anything you want if you bust your butt, and push for success!

If you learn anything from this book at all, learn this one thing: Imitate what successful people are doing! Find a mentor and hustle! I'm a living example.

Scan QR Code

Or Type the link below into your web browser
https://www.youtube.com/watch?v=XVXpUXzxQe0

CHAPTER 2

Defeat Extinction by Growing Your Army and Equipping Your Soldiers with the Right Weapons!

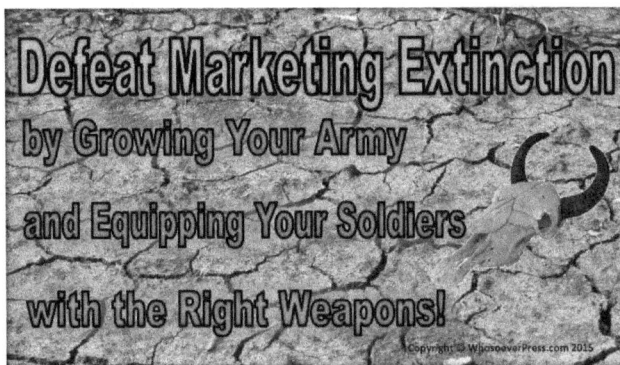

Imagine you're on the battlefield and you sense the enemy's presence. It's as though you can feel them watching you. Then you hear a cannon fire, and bullets start blazing past your head. The battle is very real, and as you glance across the field, you see the enemy charging straight at you. You've fought a good fight, and been successful in many of the smaller battles, but now a war is inevitable! Their leader is powerful and strong with millions of soldiers marching for victory. They will conquer and destroy anything and everything that gets in their way; including you. If you plan to win, it's time to rise!

As someone with a product or service to sell, you need a massive army to attract exposure. You must advance to gain massive attention. I've heard it said many times that money follows attention, and you must demand the attention of those you encounter if you expect to sell them on your product. You must focus on increasing attention for your product or service.

LET'S GET DIGITAL!

Go ahead and throw out the concept of "Word of Mouth" because this can also kill you! You must not wait for others to spread the word on what you're about. You need to do that yourself! You need to be smarter than those charging in your direction.

You need to be on Twitter and Facebook!

1. Twitter
2. Facebook

There are many Social Media sites out there such as Linked In, HeavenUp, and many more, but today I will focus on Twitter and Facebook. If you know of other great Social Media Platforms, then sign up! You need to work these platforms hard to make them produce results for your product. If you find it difficult to post all day long on multiple sites, then you're going to like what I'm about to teach you! Start scheduling your posts.

For *Twitter*, go to: www.TweetDeck.com. Here, you can manage your plan of attack. Create some good high quality posts related to your product or service, and prepare to fire all week long. You could also schedule your posts for the next month if you choose. I personally schedule a Tweet every hour on the hour from 6:00 am to 11:00 pm every day.

Twitter is an awesome place to share links to your material around the web. This gives you a chance to fire back at the enemy as they charge across the field in your direction! One thing I've learned about Twitter though, is you should post your content repeatedly due to the fact that so many people are on there. The majority of your content will just fly by, not giving anyone a chance to really check it out. Make sure you share your content repeatedly throughout the week.

Always place a link to your website or blog even if you simply just share a picture. NEVER post on Twitter without adding a link to your website. You want to push as many people as possible to your website.

Twitter is just one weapon of attack in your arsenal. When you develop a constant presence on Twitter, you will secure more followers, more people will visit your links, and you will get attention that leads to sales!

Facebook is great as well, but in my opinion, Facebook is more of a holdback, than a Sales Generator. Most people on Facebook want exactly what it says, Friends! They aren't worried about buying your product or service. They just want to say they have you on their Facebook friends list. Some of the groups may be beneficial, if you can find one, but I haven't had that experience. Facebook is great though for connecting with your supporters/fans. They love that they can message you, but rarely ever will it convert to sales. Facebook ads in my opinion do not convert to sales either. I spent well over $1,000.00 in 2014, and my ROI was $0.00. I do suggest that you create multiple pages on Facebook to promote yourself, your product and services, etc.... They may produce some sales, but the important thing with pages is they show up in Google Search results. When people search for your type of products or services, on Google or Bing you have better chances of being found!

If you're an author with multiple books, you need to have a Facebook page for each book. If the book has been out for a while now, you still need to keep your fans engaged. Engaged fans are buyers! If you're currently writing a new book, you had better have a Facebook page for that book! Post previews from the book, excerpts, video book trailers, or anything related to the book. It's never too early to start promoting a new project. If you don't have time to post on all these platforms every day, then schedule out your posts.

Don't know how to schedule a post?

Type your post out like you normally would, but instead of hitting the Publish button, click the arrow to the right. A drop down menu will appear, and give you some options. Click on schedule. There you go! You could literally take one day and schedule all of your posts for the week or even the month across all of your Social Media Platforms. Of course, if something cool pops up throughout the month, then post that too. Scheduling your posts will free up much of your time throughout the month that you can direct to other projects.

LET'S GET PHYSICAL!

Don't be afraid to spend some money! There is only so much you can do for free. Trust me on this, because I've grown my company past the three year statistic for new business start-ups by doing it with no advertising budget! I did anything and everything I could do to get free advertising and publicity. It worked for me, but now I've reached the point that I need to invest money back into my company if I want to reach the next level. I also started my company with no money. People who say it takes money to make money is out of touch with reality. They have no clue how to use money as a weapon. When I spend money, I don't want to pay big money to get little results. After researching like crazy, I discovered the key to advertising effectively! You may not believe this, but it's not in billboards! Can you sense my humor? The key to advertising is in printed promotional items.

As this section suggests, let's get physical. You need physical items going out into the market place with your brand clearly visible. It's almost like a smoke screen to the approaching enemy soldiers. They thought you were just a small puny group of locals, but they soon realize that you're everywhere. There's nowhere they can hide! Retreating isn't even an option at this point. Trust me when I say this: it's way cheaper to buy and distribute free of charge some promo product then it is to pay thousands of dollars advertising in printed media. Don't get me wrong. Printed media is awesome when it's free! Only pay for printed media as a last resort. Yes, you may get some response from printed magazine ads, and newspaper ads. You may get response from radio advertisements as well, but remember, you are trying to grow an army to defeat an enemy, not feed someone else's army. Who is the enemy anyway? The enemy is not the competition! Competition will always exist. The enemy is **extinction**. People must know you exist if you expect to survive!

Now understand this: When you pay for advertisements, your ad will run, and then it's over, whether you got any sales or not. It's over! With printed promotional products, you give it away, but it never ends like the radio, or printed ads in magazines and newspapers. Your promo product is used by your potential customer over and over while they continually see your message. They constantly walk around with you on their mind. Did you catch that? What kind of promo item am I talking about? A hat! Of course! On their mind? Now you're getting it!

"You need massive attention everywhere, not a massive billboard somewhere."

~Nate Fortner

Understand that your promo product becomes your walking billboard everywhere your soldiers march. Do you see now how to grow your army? Be creative. I'm the owner of WhosoeverPress.com, and we are a small time Christian Publishing House, and we don't have an advertising budget.

We print bookmarks with our information on them, and we ship these out to Libraries nationwide totally free to them. They place a bookmark in each book that's checked out, and guess who gets the free promotion and advertising? You got it! WhosoeverPress.com.

So, now that you realize you need tons of promo products, I want you to call our office here in Boaz, AL. at 256-706-3315.

At Whosoever Press, we have started our very own promotional product line, so we can help authors, singers and business owners achieve success! As the Captain of your army, you must equip your soldiers with the proper weapons of attack in today's market, or you will become extinct!

"Success is within the realm of possibility for those not afraid to chase their dreams."

~Nate Fortner

Scan QR Code

Or Type the link below into your web browser
https://www.youtube.com/watch?v=ChxgthOzmwg

CHAPTER 3

Remembering the days Before Internet Marketing?

Get back to the basics of offline marketing and advertising. Before the days of the internet, our world seemed much bigger. Do you remember the days before Facebook and Twitter when we actually went out door to door to advertise our offers? I remember as a child when all the vacuum cleaning salesmen would come knocking. Where has this gone? One such example is hanging up flyers around town. Here's a list of a few places where you can hang flyers to help you get back to the basics. Going back to the basics in our current day will give you an advantage against the competition, because they have stopped operating in the basics.

1. Subway Stations
2. School Offices
3. Senior Citizen Centers
4. College dormitories - hallways and restrooms
5. Churches
6. Local community clubs and organizations
7. Laundry mats
8. Apartment buildings
9. Telephone poles - especially a day or two before large city events
10. Community activity centers
11. Grocery stores bulletin boards
12. Shopping malls
13. Car Washes
14. Hotel lobbies
15. Doctor's offices
16. Gas station counters
17. Public Libraries
18. Your local Chamber of Commerce
19. Waiting rooms at car repair and tire shops
20. Highway rest areas
21. Banks

Scan QR Code

Or Type the link below into your web browser
https://www.youtube.com/watch?v=wWF_h8_S5W0

CHAPTER 4

What Is An Author's Platform?

What is an author's platform? **With whom are you engaging?** What is it that you do that gets you massive exposure and attention? Who are you influencing? The platform is simply your realm of influence.

For example, if you are a Pastor, your platform is basically your church. You are influencing a congregation of people to follow what you teach. If you are a singer, then your platform is your music. You are influencing fans to buy your albums. These people like what you have and will go to great lengths to hear what you have to say. This is your platform.

However, just because you may have a platform, doesn't mean you know how to produce a sale. As an author, your product is your book, but before people buy it, they want to know that it's worth the price. Anyone can write a book. It's how you stand out that gets you the sale.

What authority do you have to write a book? What credentials do you have? If you're a nonfiction author, and your writing gives advice on a particular subject, what gives you the right to do so? What experience or education do you have on this subject? Do you have a degree in that field, or are you just looking for a lucky streak? People want quality, and if you can't provide that for them, they'll move on.

How many people are you reaching? How many sales are you producing? How many people have subscribed to your email list? (*Mailchimp.com*)

How Do You Grow Your Platform If You Are Just Starting Out?

First, you need to identify your target market. Who is your crowd of readers, and how and where can you engage with them?

Try creating and distributing quality content. Write some articles or short stories and take them, or email them to your local media outlets such as newspapers, television, and radio. This doesn't guarantee you results, but it can't hurt you. You'll be starting the process of presenting yourself as a professional in your field. Include your name and contact information on this one page article and offer to appear as a guest on their show for an interview.

You have no excuse for not doing this. It's easy and only costs you about a dollar, if that! Be sure to include in your signature that you're the author of "Your Book Title." If you can afford it, send a free autographed copy of your book as well.

For more information on building your author platform, check out this great site:
www.janefriedman.com/2012/03/13/author-platform-definition

Get FREE access to the world's largest list of Magazines and Newspapers on the planet.

Visit: www.World-Newspapers.com

Scan QR Code

Or Type the link below into your web browser
https://www.youtube.com/watch?v=nkpACqx3zWw

CHAPTER 5

The Dollar Is Bouncing Back From Poverty

According to the Washington Post, the euro has fallen to a 12-year low of $1.07, down from $1.39 just last year. So with a stronger dollar, doesn't that mean our economy is getting stronger? Of course, it does! Business is booming in the US, and we have all started to get back to our normal lives again, the way it was before the recession. With the majority of the European countries still trying to get their finances in order, the US has the ball in its court. However, this could mean interest rates may soon be on the rise.

So what does this mean for the publishing industry? At this point, it may be too soon to tell. For the self-published author, prices may be going up on publishing packages and promotional products. However, the good side is royalties should also go up. As always, be creative and look to gain massive exposure. Do your part to get more of the American dollar while it's worth it.

CHAPTER 6

Why You Need to Market

It would be nice if all you had to do was write. Then you could let somebody else handle all of that "marketing" stuff. Unfortunately, the reality is that you will have to do it yourself. This is true even if you have a contract with a major publisher. They do the work to get your book into bookstores, but the rest is up to you. Sometimes you even have to be the one to actually convince the bookstores to carry your book.

Want to do a book tour? You are booking it yourself most of the time. This means getting on the phone with the bookstores yourself. My first book tour, I scheduled myself!

You can't expect your customers to come to you. You have to go to your customers. There are a lot of books out there right now. A whole lot of them. People must know you exist. You can talk about niches all you want, but there are already books in your niche available.

So how do you make your book stand out from all of those other books? **You must be ready do marketing, promoting, branding, cold calling, sending emails, and the list goes on and on.** You cannot deny the fact that you have to get attention for you product or service.

Your readers aren't just buying your book. They are buying a bit of you. The book comes with a story beyond what is in its pages. It comes with your story.

You need to make your readers care about not only the book but the author as well. If you are writing fiction this means that they think you are an interesting person with an interesting story to tell. If you are writing non-fiction this means that you want people to believe that you are an expert on your topic.

However, marketing is not just about telling your story. It is about getting potential readers to take action. Learning to write persuasive sales copy is an important part of the book marketing process.

The last reason is you need to market:

As a self-publishing author, you probably have already realized that no one else is going to market your book for you. This applies equally to traditionally published books as well.

You must take massive action in marketing and promoting your book if you expect it to go anywhere.

Scan QR Code

Or Type the link below into your web browser
https://www.youtube.com/watch?v=V1OGBuCsv_Y

CHAPTER 7

Determining Your Audience

Have you defined your target audience? Do you know what they are looking for? It will make the marketing process much easier if you start with marketing in mind before the book is even written.

This applies to fiction and non-fiction equally.

Whether you are writing a short how-to guide as a Kindle book or a hundred thousand word epic novel, your target market is not "everybody." Even for best-sellers, the target audience is not everybody. There are people who cannot stand Stephen King's writing. There are people that gag at the thought of opening a book by Nicholas Sparks. Yet we are all envious of their success. They write mega-bestsellers, even with targeting "everybody."

Just because a book is written for a particular audience doesn't mean that they will be the only ones who read it. If it is well written, then your target audience will want everybody to read it.

Think of Harry Potter. Who was the target audience for the first Harry Potter book? If you said 10 year old boys, then you are our big winner. Now, are ten year old boys the only people reading Harry Potter? Hardly. You are not limited by your target audience, but you still need one to focus on.

Scan QR Code

Or Type the link below into your web browser
https://www.youtube.com/watch?v=Y5-lcjzmqYY

CHAPTER 8

Your Website

Get a website. You need to have one as an author and preferably you should have a separate one for each book. Web hosting is cheap. If you are the Do-It-Youself type, you can get a single shared hosting plan and host multiple websites under the same plan. Check out www.Weebly.com for a free website, or www.IXWebhosting.com for a paid platform to host multiple sites.

If you do not have website coding skills, you can easily find somebody. I recommend finding a local web development company. You can also find individuals at Meetups in your area. If you can't do that or you are REALLY on a tight budget you can find freelancers online. The quality of site you will get is mixed and good communication is important. Remember that not all of them write and read as well as you. Their skills are in computers, not communications. The cheap ones will barely speak any English.

What are some of the things that need to be on your website?

You need a biography, preferably with a picture.

You need information about your book or books.

You need a calendar of events for your book promotions (if you are running any).

You need links to your Facebook and Twitter pages.

You need a blog on your site, or a link to your blog.

You need a way to build your email list.

Let's focus on the last one.

How do you do that? Sign up for a list service. I recommend MailChimp.com. Sign up instructions are on their site. They are one of the easiest to use and integrate into your website. An email list provider will make sure you stay on the right side of Spam rules. Have you ever had to click a confirmation link to confirm you want to be on somebody's email list? That is the purpose of the list provider.

You want to keep in touch with your fans. An email list is the way to do it. Not everybody is on every social media account. Some people aren't on social media at all. Almost everybody in the world has at least one email account.

Now what do you do with your email list? An email list is long-term marketing. I am fond of saying that you can't eat an email list. However, you aren't just stopping with one book, are you? You want to be able to market all of your books to your audience. After all, if they liked one then they are more likely to like the others.

Are the people on your email list knowledgeable marketers? Maybe some of them are? If you are selling your book on Amazon (and you certainly should be) then remind your readers that if they promote your book through the Amazon Affiliate program, they can earn a percentage of the sales they drive your way.

They get money. You get money and readers. Everybody wins.

What else should you have on your website?

It goes without saying, that you should have links to where people can buy your books. Somehow, this is not addressed as it should be. If you are selling on Amazon, make sure the links are affiliate links so that you can earn a little extra from each sale. Amazon explicitly allows this.

CHAPTER 9

Miscellaneous Low Cost Ideas to Promote Your Book

Here are a few simple ideas for increasing your marketing reach. Some are more traditional marketing techniques, while others rely on the web and some technical skills. If you don't have the technical skills you can easily contract out portions of the work.

Press releases

Write a press release. It is simple and low cost, so why not? Maybe it will get picked up by somebody if your book is on a timely topic; probably not, though. The world is flooded with press releases and the vast majority of them are completely ignored.

Should you pay somebody to write a press release for you? Unless your book is on a very timely topic it is highly unlikely that you will get your money back. As I said, odds are the press release will be ignored. However, on the off chance that it manages to catch somebody's attention you should write one.

When can a press release work? **A press release can sometimes work if it is on a timely topic and you can present yourself as an expert on that topic.** This is why you have to do a lot of personal brand marketing even before the book is released. If you can position yourself as an expert, then you have a much better chance of getting your press release picked up.

It also helps if you can get press coverage from other people on your own. Even if it's a small, local press, it can help. That kind of validation makes members of the press feel safe in covering you. If others have done it then you must be okay.

Submit your Press Release for FREE to the websites listed below!

www.PRLog.org
www.Free-Press-Release.com

Reviews

Reviews are important for marketing in several ways. If the review is from a reader with no incentive to write the review, that is the most powerful review of all.

Is it dishonest to pay for reviews? The general rule of thumb is that it is dishonest to pay for reviews. There are mixed opinion on whether or not you can pay for honest reviews.

Giving books away for reviewers is a standard technique that the big publishing houses use. The honest reviewer will disclose that they received a copy of the book for free.

Host a Book Release Party

It may just be friends and family that show, but everybody loves a good party. At the very minimum it will get them talking about your book. Your family and friends will be your very first advocates. They know people. They know people that you do not know. They can spread the word about your book.

Give them all free signed copies. This is why you want appeal editions of your book, remember?

This is another reason why you want to make your book the very best it can be. If you want your family and friends to market your book for you then you don't want to embarrass them. They do not want to recommend a lousy book to their friends.

Videos

For better or for worse, the Internet thrives on videos. People like their videos. If you want to market to them you need to be able to release videos. YouTube.com is a great video publishing platform. If you need a video book trailer produced for your book, then visit WhosoeverPress.com. The internet is full of potential readers, they just need to know your book exists! Video book trailers are great! You could also start a video series.

Slideshare

If your book is non-fiction then there is nothing easier than creating a simple PowerPoint presentation about your topic. Make it information dense so the reader is getting real value out of it. Mention your book at the very beginning and at the very end.

Then post the presentation on Slideshare.com It is a website dedicated to sharing slideshows. What makes a good presentation? It must be complete. None of this "for the answer, read my book." People will click off the page before they even finish reading that sentence.

Make a webinar

This is a video on steroids. Take the presentation that you just made and create a whole half hour long presentation from it. Mention your book once at the beginning and once at the end. Don't make it a half hour long sales pitch.

You can do a LIVE webinar and record it or, you can just record a webinar type video at home and then upload it to your website. This is what I recommend for beginners until you get really good at pacing your presentations.

Fortunately for you, making the videos is easy. Most laptops come with web cams already built in. Visit Ustream.com and create an account. Ustream.com is an awesome online platform where you can share your webinar directly with your social media accounts. I have used this site on multiple occasions.

QR Codes

Want to create your own Free QR Codes? You can create as many as you wish free of charge at:
www.goqr.me

Scan QR Code

Or Type the link below into your web browser
https://www.youtube.com/watch?v=9vb_hpGi2eA

CHAPTER 10

Cracking the Article Writing Code

You can write articles on the topic of your book and post them around the web. Again, this makes the most sense for non-fiction books. It also works for fiction if there is a central theme in your story.

How-to sites are the easiest and most popular sites to submit your work. You need to be creating content on the web that will push people back to your website. Use SEO (Search Engine Optimization) or Keywords and key phrases to connect your content.

Many times you will not get paid for these contributions. If you are not making money directly, make sure that you get a link to your site. Preferably, the link will be indexed by Google and will help the search engine rankings of your main site. You may also write articles, and submit them to Nate@WhosoeverPress.com to be considered for publication in the Whosoever Press Magazine.

There are so many article submission sites around the web that I could list, but here's a few that pay cash to help you get stared.

1. www.CatholicDigest.com/writes_guidelines.html
2. www.EarthIsland.org/journal/index.php/guidelines
3. www.VQRonline.org/about-vqr/submissions

4. www.outdoors.org/publications/outdoors/contributor-guidelines.cfm

   You can also get FREE access to over 100 websites that will pay you to write articles by visiting WritersInCharge.com. Sign up with your email, and get instant access to the full list.

CHAPTER 11

Overnight Success as a Writer

Is writing your hobby or passion? Do you see yourself as a writer by profession? These are very interesting questions that people who are interested in writing can answer. If you are the type of person who always wrote stuff in your diary, pieces of paper, tissue paper, or any writing material, just to get your thoughts out, then you might be a writer in the making. Becoming a writer is not an easy task. There are many successful writers who have taken years to polish their crafts and may not be getting their "big breaks." It is a daunting task, but it will give you the highest satisfaction in life if you fulfill your lifelong dream of being a writer. Getting there will be the hard part. Getting published is the ultimate validation of a writer and having your books read by people is the fulfillment of that dream. Many famous writers never imagined the magnitude of their words on people who are reading their books and the impact those words have on the lives of their readers. Some of them scribbled their thoughts on scraps of paper or even pieces of tissue paper while drinking tea in a café or while traveling home on a train. They never thought that their creation would ever reach the farthest places on earth, but it did. Their thoughts did fly out, and it reached millions of people. Their works of art inspired and sparked something in people from around the world. Their daily musings about life were shared by millions, and these musings turned into famous quotes and inspirational texts that many are using.

No one can ever say what your words can do unless you put them on paper. Yes, you can give inspirational talks and speeches, but you also need to etch them on paper so you can pass them on to others. Many speeches and well-said talks began with writing and these words became famous because they were made available in print form. So, if you are a person who has ideas and thoughts bursting from your head, write it on something and keep writing. If you want to know how to become an overnight success, then read, read, read and learn a thing or two about the world of written words.

Scan QR Code

Or Type the link below into your web browser
https://www.youtube.com/watch?v=RZ5xHkV9R1U

CHAPTER 12

Creating Quality Do-It-Yourself Marketing Content

Let's get personal. I'm the owner of Whosoever Press. I've been running my company since August of 2012. Yes, we are a new company, but most new companies that are bound to fail, do so within the first three years. We have beat the statistics! Do we have it all figured out? Not exactly! We have published approximately 10 authors, and we are still growing. Like all new start-ups, we have faced our fair share of obstacles, but we're making it happen. From what I can see taking place in the lives of authors everywhere, unless you have a ton of money to advertise, then books aren't flying off the shelves. Okay, well we could always buy some cheap books on Marketing, and take the "Do-It-Yourself" route. Seriously? If you have tried this, then you have already realized there are not very many good books out there! Most of the Marketing & Promotion books that I have read are all basic beginners' guides that offer little to no real help. Honestly, most of it is just fluff! If I'm going to do it myself, I want to buy a book that contains addresses, phone numbers, personal contacts, emails, and explanations on how to do it step-by-step. It's easy to publish a Kindle, and offer it for $0.99. You may even sale a ton of copies, but guess what? Once the bad reviews start rolling in, then your hot book that sold 10 copies dies completely. Although, it may not be what you want to hear right now, it is so very true. Content is king! Let me help you better understand this concept. For example, say you are an author who writes about such a small niche, that there are only 100 authors total writing about this subject matter.

Your marketing program is not to squash the competition, but rather to lead the competition. Be the top expert in your niche. No, you may not be the smartest on the subject, but if you are pumping out tons of content, then guess who is going to be seen? Exactly! You! If there are 100 authors in the same niche, and 50 are blogging and 50 aren't, guess who is going to get more attention? Exactly! The 50% who are blogging. Now, let's say 40% of the 50% are also posting YouTube videos. Then, only 10% of the 40% are writing press releases each week and submitting them to newspapers and magazines. Let's say you are in the top 5% because you do all of the above, but in addition, you also call bookstores each week introducing yourself to the owners asking to do a book signing at their store. Out of all these groups of people, who do you think will move more books?

It doesn't necessarily matter who is doing more here and there. If you want to be successful, you must gain attention! That means constantly producing quality content. One video, one Press Release, one book, or one book signing will not produce long lasting results! Sorry, but it won't work! Now, look at it like this: Out of 100 people trying to promote their book, you need to stand out, but how? Again, it's all about content! Blogging is FREE! No, it may not produce the results you want at first, but here's the thing. Each time you post a blog, when you insert your keywords for SEO (Search Engine Optimization), this blog will eventually be tagged to your name and the subject you're writing about online. So, to better explain this, go to: www.Google.com and type your name into the search bar. This is an easy way to see what's floating around about you online. Each time you post a blog, and use good keywords and phrases, your blog posts will start showing up. Okay, so now, you want to tag your blogs with the subject you're writing about, so when people search that subject online, your blog postings start showing up! It truly works, if you do it properly. Like I mentioned earlier though, you can't just publish one post or one video. You need to flood the internet with quality content on the subject you write about. Also, on your website, place links to your blog posts on the internet. Don't forget to put links in your blog posts pushing people to your website. Links are very important to get people going where you want them to go. Go to: www.YouTube.com and type in the subject you write about, and see what comes up. You need to be producing videos and tagging them appropriately to get them showing up when people are searching for your type of content.

The whole point of this:

#1 Create Quality Content

#2 Train Others

#3 Push People to your website where they can purchase you book(s)

#4 Get your name out there

#5 I could continue on & on

Here's a few tips:

1. Start Blogging for free at: http://www.Blogger.com You may also choose to use: http://www.WordPress.com

2. Start posting videos now at: http://www.YouTube.com You may also choose to use: http://www.Vimeo.com

3. Learn what Keywords & Key Phrases are by searching "Keywords and Key Phrases" on http://www.YouTube.com

4. Are you a Christian writer? Post videos on: http://www.GodTube.com

5. Search Google for: "Local Newspapers" Get the address and stop by. Take your book with you. Walk in and ask to speak with a Reporter. Tell them you want to speak with someone about doing a Press Release. In my experience, if they have a reporter available, they'll do a free interview on the spot.

These tips are not fluff, and they will truly help to start pushing you in the right direction!

I challenge you to start creating some serious content, and start driving people to your website!

Need a Publisher? Visit: http://www.WhosoeverPress.com

At: http://www.WhosoeverPress.com be sure to visit The Author Zone and get tons of free ideas and articles! Do you have tips and ideas that have proven helpful to you? Submit them to: Nate@WhosoeverPress.com

Also visit: www.TheAuthorZoneLearningCenter.com

When I first started traveling as an author a few years back, I understood that I needed to be creating content. I knew that I had to get information out online about my book. Even though they are so basic and simple, check out these videos below. When I went to a new town, I would film a video at the bookstore the day of, or somewhere in town few days ahead of time. Once I had my video, I paid Facebook to promote my video geographically pinpointing the viewership to the surrounding towns. I wanted people to know I was there, and they needed to come buy my book. Plus, as a YouTube Partner, I get paid when people watch my content. It was another awesome benefit to creating the content. Does quality matter with your videos? I'd say do the best you can, but when creating content, quantity will always be what gets people's attention. Quantity over quality. You can also visit: www.Google.com/Adwords and create an account to start promoting and advertising your video on YouTube.

Scan QR Code
Or Type the link below into your web browser
https://www.youtube.com/watch?v=dIhjCYbNEAo

Scan QR Code

Or Type the link below into your web browser
https://www.youtube.com/watch?v=L1fC9OROowc

Scan QR Code

Or Type the link below into your web browser
https://www.youtube.com/watch?v=aAuJl1-P9Wc

Scan QR Code

Or Type the link below into your web browser
https://www.youtube.com/watch?v=FWuUejnxyul

Scan QR Code

Or Type the link below into your web browser
https://www.youtube.com/watch?v=iB9AQ19Cx-M

CHAPTER 13

How Can I Make More Money?

Now, that's a bright idea!

As an author, I want to sell more books. I want my fans to read what I write. I want my books to be popular and become Best-Sellers. As a Singer, I want to write songs that people will want to sing along with in their cars. I want to turn on the radio and hear myself singing. I want to be a success in the music world. As a Publisher, I want everyone I publish to be successful! I want them out doing what they love, and getting paid! The one thing that we all face is the fact that most of us lack the money it takes to be able to give up our day job. The question we all want the answer to is: *How do we get more sales?*

You can pay for advertisements and TV commercials. You could also drop a couple thousand dollars and advertise in your favorite magazine. The possibilities are endless to the amount of ways you could choose to throw your money around. I've been running my company WhosoeverPress.com for three years totally debt free and paid very little in advertising dollars. I admit I'm at a point where if I expect to grow, I'm going to have to fork out some money to promote, but the point is, I made it three years debt free, no advertising budget, and started out with no money! Yeah, I've heard the old quote as well. "It takes money to make money!" Honestly, that's a load of bull! All you need is an idea to make money!

I started my second business about 2 years into my first business. The first year, I had the idea, and I sold a local business owner on the idea. I would provide for them a need that they were already paying for, and I would give it to them for free! They loved my idea! Yes, the first year was a rough start up since I was doing it debt free, and with no advertising dollars, but I did it! 2015 is the second year I've been running this business, and I've provided this product for the local business totally free all year long! I can't even begin to tell you how much money I've saved this local business. Not only did this idea of mine save this company money, I made money, and other businesses all over town have made money off of my idea. I did it all debt free and with no advertising budget. Again, all you need to make money is an idea!

HOW DID I DO IT?

Of course, social media played a major role in my success. On the other hand, my first paying job actually came through a free advertising platform here in my local town. I placed a free ad in a local sales magazine. Taking the time to do this made me $600.00 on my first phone call. Yes, I had to work hard to up hold my end of the deal, but I did it well. As this author grew in success and fame, many newspaper articles were written about his book, and guess who received free publicity? That's right. www.WhosoeverPress.com!

I've heard it said many times that most new Start-Up Companies fail within their first three years. I've beat the statistics! It has not been easy. Don't quit your day job until you're making enough money to supplement your income. You will probably make mistakes along the way as well, but as long as you earn from your mistakes, these will serve as building blocks for you.

HOW DO YOU MEASURE SUCCESS?

We all measure success differently, but the one thing we all want is more sales. The answer is not simple. It's not easy, and it won't happen overnight. However, if you work hard, you can achieve success. To be completely honest with you, you need to become Omnipresent! You need to be everywhere at the same time. You need to be on every social media platform you can find, and working it hard. I've heard some people say it's better to only be on 1 or 2 social media platforms and run them well, rather than being on 12 and running them all poorly. While I agree with that knowledge, that is an excuse to fail! Take at least one day a week to schedule your posts on Facebook. Create multiple pages on Facebook, and schedule your posts. Go to www.Tweetdeck.com and start scheduling your weekly posts for Twitter. Twitter is a very powerful platform for getting your content in front of your potential customers. Possibly even someone who would be interested in buying your product or service. Do some research and start using #Hashtags if you aren't already. Since I started using #Hashtags on Twitter, I have gotten tons more response from my posts. Another website I use is TweetJulebox.com. I have a paid monthly subscription which allows me to promote each of my authors multiple times daily just on Twitter alone.

To Sum it all up, you need to be creating news every day. Don't wait to be discovered because that will probably never happen. You must put yourself in front of those that you want to know you exist. You need to be blogging, creating YouTube videos, on every Social Media Platform you can find! If you spend money an advertising, test the waters, and spend your dollar wisely! One thing that I have personally had great success with is YouTube ads. When You Tube plays my video as an ad before another video. You can literally pin point your video ad to a geographical location on the earth, and YouTube will make it happen for you. I'm not exaggerating when I say this at all, but every time I have ever run a major campaign on YouTube, I've always had someone message me, call me, text me, or someone to tell me they saw my video ad. You must be creating content and getting some publicity if you expect people to know who you are.

It may seem like a stretch, but reach out to your local newspaper, and ask if you can write a column each week on your topic. A little hint: Most local papers have an opinions section. You can write an Opinion article and submit it for review. Just be sure to add your Signature. Not just your name, but your name, website, author of "Your Book Title" etc...

Start Making Some Noise! Start Making Some More Money!

CHAPTER 14

A Bad Cover Will Cost You Sales

We've all heard the famous line, "Don't judge a book by its cover." The truth is, your book WILL BE JUDGED by its cover. You will lose sales because you have a bad or misleading cover design. If you're a self-published author, then you first have to overcome the stigma that your book sucks because it's poor quality and full of grammatical errors. You need top quality so readers won't second guess your writing.

First, you need a professional looking book cover. Second, your back cover description must engage the reader. On your back cover design, your description needs to excite the buyer and push them to fork over the cash and buy your book. Thirdly, you know someone who may possibly buy your book is going to flip through the pages. Your book's interior must look phenomenal!

Covers will vary in price, but if you want an awesome cover, call our office! 256-706-3315. I'll give you a $500.00 book cover for only $300.00. If you just need a digital Kindle front cover, then I'll make yours standout for only $150.00.

One author who is now with my company, published her book with another well-known publisher, and her cover kept her book from selling. After she made the transition to WhosoeverPress.com, her new format and book cover dramatically increased her book's selling potential.

Need a cover design?

Call WhosoeverPress.com 256-706-3315

We'll make you look so good, people will want to buy your promotional flyers!

CHAPTER 15

Adjusting the Price of Your Book

The more you promote your book, regardless of your genre, the more the book will sell. The awesome thing is for those authors who have multiple books. As one book picks up momentum, your other books will start selling more as well. Even if you focus on pushing one book, and dump tons of money on advertising, your other books will begin to sell.

The #1 reason why your books aren't selling is simply because people don't know who you are. You must demand attention if you want your books to sell. Make it your daily goal to introduce yourself to ten or more new people. Give them a business card, and ask to do business with them in the future. If you need business cards, visit WhosoeverPress.com or call 256-706-3315. Mention that you're reading this book, and I'll give you 5,000 full color Double-sided UV laminate protected cards for only $100.00. You'll pay over $500.00 anywhere else for this quality and quantity.

Another valuable tip is to price your book higher than you originally thought. For example, a Paperback book of 250 pages needs to be priced for at least $20.00. If it's a 250 page Hardback book, you need to price it at least $25.00 to $30.00. You have to start showing people that your work is valuable, and that the price they pay for the book is not just a cost, but an investment into their lives.

Another reason to set a higher MSRP is because bookstores will want between 40% - 60% off of this price. You will end up losing what little bit of royalty you deserve from the sale. Push like freaking crazy so your books will get the attention they deserve!

CHAPTER 16

My Take on Network Marketing

Joining your local Chamber of Commerce is the easiest way to mingle with other business owners in your town and surrounding cities. It may seem like a waste of time, but I assure you, you need to be growing your network of influence. Have plenty of business cards on hand, and make sure you introduce yourself to every single person in the room, giving each of them your card. You may be reading this and saying to yourself, *"I'm not a business owner, I'm an author."* As an author, your book is your business, and you must treat it like one if you expect it to grow!

Most Chambers of Commerce have at least one monthly meeting to allow the members to network. Many times, if you're not a go-getter like me, your business will only be a success because of the people you know. Many times, , it's still not enough to sustain you. In other words, if you want to survive, find a business clique and get involved. Make sure that when someone needs your product or type of service, you are the first person who comes to their mind!

You must learn early on that "No" really means "Yes," and you must be willing to relentlessly pursue new avenues to create success whether people like you or not. Most people say, "No" simply because they don't "know" you, or enough about your product to make an informed decision about doing business with you. Get out of obscurity, and make sure people know you and your name. Brand yourself with the company you run. You need to follow up with all those "No's" and hit them over and over until they buy.

According to GrantCardone.com

48% of sales people never follow up with a prospect.

25% of sales people make a second contact and stop.

12% of sales people only make three contacts and stop.

Only 10% of sales people make more than three contacts.

2% of sales are made on the first contact.

3% of sales are made on the second contact.

5% of sales are made on the third contact.

10% of sales are made on the fourth contact.

80% of sales are made on the fifth to twelfth contact.

It's important to understand that networking will help you to expand your reach of influence pretty quickly, but you need to stay in touch with people.

For authors, you need to understand these statistics above when you pitch your book(s) to bookstore owners.

Why should we network anyway?

Answer: NOT ENOUGH PEOPLE KNOW WHO YOU ARE!

CHAPTER 17

Partnership Marketing

What is Partnership Marketing? Here's my personal definition: *"The act of directing ones clients to another's business for commerce."* In Boaz, AL. where I live, I run a Publishing Company called WhosoeverPress.com. Not only do we Publish books, but we have our own Promotional Product Line. We provide everything our authors will need to promote their books. This also provides another stream of income for my company. Yes, we provide our promotional products for anyone to purchase, not just our authors. Call my office right now, and I'll make you look so great on paper, people will want to purchase your promo flyers!

I have another side to my company as well, in which we sell advertisements to local businesses. I created a solution for a local company in need of a product, by actually providing the product for them totally free. I can't even tell you how much money I've saved this company. Tons! How did I provide it to them free of charge you're wondering? I sold advertisements that I literally printed on the product. When Company A uses the product, Company B gets their advertisement into circulation. Thousands and thousands of people see their advertisement guaranteed! What happened behind the scenes, was I worked out an agreement with Company A, that if I provided their product for them for free, they would get their logo on the front, and other businesses could advertise on the back. Company

A originally didn't even have their own logo on the product. Company A agreed, and I started selling advertisements. Company A moves 750 to 1,000 products in our community of approximately 10,000 people every single week. Company A gets a huge amount of foot traffic from surrounding towns as well, so Company A never runs out of new customers. I have businesses constantly calling me wanting to advertise! In my opinion, this is a lot easier than going out trying to sell the ads, and the product is literally placed into the hands of Company A's customers. Now Company B has mini billboards walking around all over town!

The key to making this an even bigger success is when I sell advertisements to Company B, they place an exclusive offer in their ad. They push their customers to Company A to buy Company A's product in exchange for a coupon to get their own product at a cheaper rate. This is a tremendous way to grow local businesses, especially in a small town! This in a nutshell is cross-promotion between businesses. Let me say this as well, Company A sells a high dollar product that everyone wants every single day! Minimum wage workers save their money to buy this product, and the wealthy are here 2 or 3 times per day. When Company B advertises on the product that I provide for Company A, Company B is getting their product pitched, not only to the lower class, but to the upper class as well!

I saw a creative angle in which I could provide for Company A, while helping Company B, and my bank account started smiling even more! Because of this idea, I've had many advertisers start purchasing their promotional product from my company. One such company is www.AdvancedAngler.com

The owner of the company was so impressed with my idea on Coffee Sleeve Marketing that now, he tells coffee shops everywhere how they can get free coffee sleeves if they just call me. Be sure to help me say thanks, and purchase your fishing products from www.AdvancedAngler.com.

In this life, you will be remembered for one of two things, the problems you created, and the problems you solved. Be a Problem Solver!

"You need massive attention everywhere, not a massive billboard somewhere!"

~Nate Fortner

Nate Fortner, Author of, *"Book Marketing in the 21st Century,"* and *"How to be a Successful Writer Overnight."*

CHAPTER 18

Poor Is No Excuse!

Slow down and take a break. You work way too hard and too much. Enjoy yourself a little bit. I personally hate being told to slow down because it infuriates me when the people closest to me don't understand my drive. Growing up poor, I know what it's like to not have enough money. I remember as a kid, the only time we went out for French fries or ice cream was on Wednesday nights after church because it was free for Kids Club members. Without even telling you the name of the next restaurant, we ate at the Captain's house every Thursday evening because kids ate free. I now hate seafood. I can't stand the smell of fish. I want to hurl when I smell the scent of dead fish.

Growing up poor has played such a major role in my life to push for success. I want success in my life. I want success for my family, my business, my church, and in every aspect of my life. I've been told by countless people that they admire my ambition, and go-getter attitude, but tell me I need to slow down because I make people nervous. I'm committed to success, and I'll never stop reaching for my goals! I'm so committed to success that my blood platelets fight and push the others out of the way racing to keep me pumping at full speed. When I bleed, my blood screams winner!

I refuse to slow down or give up on my dreams! I will never stop or give up on myself. I will stay focused and committed to my success! Growing up, we were so poor that I still have the taste of Ketchup in my mouth from all the ketchup sandwiches we would eat. I know what poor looks like, but my parents struggled to make life the best it could be for my sister and me. We grew up with great parents who loved us.

Want to understand my drive? None of us are promised tomorrow. Today is all we have, so we need to make today count! Today is the day the Lord has made, and we better make it count! Success isn't free. Success isn't given. Success isn't even earned. It's made! Focus and get committed to success!

You need to have a force pushing you and driving you to achieve success. Stop crying and blaming others for why you're a loser in business. Wake up with a mindset to win and do whatever it takes!

CHAPTER 19

The Author's Pledge of Success

I refuse to slow down or give up on my dreams!

I will never stop or give up believing in myself!

I will stay focused and committed to my success!

The promise of no tomorrow will be my driving force for today!

I will not whine and blame others for my failures!

I will wake every day with a mindset to win and do whatever it takes!

Success Isn't Free! Success Isn't Given!

Success Isn't Even Earned, It's Made!

CHAPTER 20

The Broken Trap Called God

If God desires for us to be successful, then it will happen, Amen. Wrong! I do believe that God wants us to live meaningful success-filled lives, but I also believe He expects us to work for our victories. I could point you to countless stories in the Bible where God said, "Go!" I recall in the book of Genesis that God kicked Adam and Eve out of the Garden of Eden. What did He tell them? "Go!" Go and till the land, work hard and sweat. A little further in Genesis, we read the account of Noah and the Ark. God told Noah that the rain was coming, and he needed to build a boat. God gave Noah an instruction. In the New Testament, Jesus told Naaman to go dip seven times in the Jordan River before he could receive his healing. At the end of The Gospels, Jesus gives His disciples another instruction. As He's ascending into the clouds, He says, "GO!"

This is the broken mindset that has hit many Americans today, and especially lazy Christians! Before you start bashing me for calling you a lazy Christian, I used to be one to, but then, I woke up and realized that God didn't call me to be lazy. He called me to be successful in all that I set my mind to achieve. He called me to be different. He didn't create me, call me, and train me just to fit in with the crowd. Oh, wait a minute. Isn't that what He's called all Christians to do, be different? The point is, so many people, Christians or not, are blaming God for their laziness!

Laziness is a sin by the way. Thinking that God is going to magically turn everything we touch into gold is a trap. God expects you to work hard to attain success in your life. Don't fall prey to this broken trap mindset. The broken trap really isn't broken. The trap is set, the spring is loaded, and you will get caught if you don't get your head in the game! The broken trap is more of a mindset than anything. Don't think that God's just going to hand success over to you. Yes, you better be praying and asking for wisdom to make wise decisions for your business. If you fail in your business, your family will pay the price for your laziness. Get out of this trap, and stop blaming Jesus! Success Isn't Free! Success Isn't Given! Success Isn't even Earned! It's Made!

If you still believe God is going to bless your laziness, then blow the dust off of your Bible and start reading Matthew 25:14-30.

CHAPTER 21

Faith Is Overrated!

Faith without works is dead! If you have a great idea, but you fail to develop a plan of action, your faith is dead. Faith requires action! You can quote Bible verses all you want, but you're just using the Bible as an excuse to justify your laziness. Throughout the New Testament, the people Jesus healed, He gave them an instruction. He wanted to see their faith in action. Faith and action go hand in hand. Most of what people call faith is truly foolishness. Foolishness is a sin. If you quit your job without a plan of action for tomorrow's success, that's not faith, it's foolish! If you can't distinguish the difference between faith and foolishness, remember this:

Faith Requires Action & Foolishness Is Laziness!

CHAPTER 22

The Favor Factor

Favor - "To feel or show approval or preference for."

At some point in your life, you've known at least one person who has received a job, promotion, raise, or something simply because of who they were or who they knew. That's called "The Favor Factor." Whether you like the idea or not, now is the time to flip through the rolodex of your mind, and remember those who you have helped in the past. Make a list of those people, the influential people in your life, and anyone who owes you a favor. You invested in them, and now it's time for your investments to start paying some interest! This time, your ROI (return on investment) is favor!

To be quite honest, some things in life only happen for you because of who you know. "The Favor Factor" must be a part of your marketing plan. Talent is never enough. You need to reach out to the influential people in your life like your Pastor, School Principal, College Professor, the CEO of the company that employs you, or even your celebrity cousin who chills with Leo or Cruise on the weekends. It's time to dig deep, and ask for some free promotion from those who can help you make some waves. Think in Tsunami proportions! Get some hurricane force winds of favor blowing in your direction!

There have been many times in my life that had it not been for the people I knew, I'd have been sitting on the sidelines. There has always been someone more qualified, more educated, more financially feasible, or better looking, but I got the job due to the sweat-less favor of others in my life.

Use the power of "The Favor Factor" to drive book sales, and become a person of influence yourself. You must embrace this idea of getting what you deserve, and don't be afraid to ask for help from those whom you have shown favor. Most of them will be more than willing to give you a plug for your book. Most will feel honored that you asked them to be a part of helping to get your book the attention it deserves.

Having the favor of just one influential person could boost your book sales over the top. Favor will open doors that have been bolted shut for years. "The Favor Factor" will produce prosperity, protection, influence and many other advantages.

"The favor of the right person could be the weight you need to tip the scales in your direction."

~Nate Fortner

"For You, O LORD, will bless the righteous; with favor You will surround him as with a shield." (*NKJV*, Psalm 5:12).

Scan QR Code
Or Type the link below into your web browser
https://www.youtube.com/watch?v=EkQ447bYH-U

This Interview Was Only Possible Because of Favor!

CHAPTER 23

King David's Five Stones of Business Success

Many times, we forget that growing a successful business requires hard work. Success isn't free, nor does it come cheap. You may not have the wisdom of King Solomon, or the good looks of King David, but one thing you must have is determination to succeed. Most of us are familiar with the Biblical story of David and Goliath. David had just been anointed by the Prophet Samuel to be King over Israel. God was no longer pleased with King Saul as the leader over His people.

Jesse, who was David's Father, one day asked him to take some food to David's brothers who were fighting in battle against the Philistines. When David arrived, he was astonished to find the Israelite army cowering in fear, afraid of Goliath. Goliath was a giant in the land who was cussing the God of the Israelites, full of pride and ready to fight.

When the young boy David saw what was going on, he questioned the faith of the Israelite soldiers. After a meeting with King Saul, David went to the brook, picked up five round smooth stones, and marched into the valley. David yelled, "Who is this uncircumcised Philistine that defiles the name of the Lord God of Israel?" Goliath, the giant, mocked David and made fun of him. David had an obstacle in front of him, but determination and faith in God charged his spiritual battery, and he found himself running toward Goliath.

Maybe today you're facing a Goliath-sized problem in your business, and you need a David to remove the giant.

The stones David picked from the brook, were weapons to take down the obstacle. David chose five stones, but only needed one. In business, you will face obstacles from time to time. The forgotten stones are the weapons you will use to rid your business of Goliaths in your path. The biggest Goliath you will face in business will be Obscurity. Although David only needed one stone, we'll be using the four forgotten stones as well.

What Do the Five Stones Represent?

Stone#1: Product
Stone#2: Marketing & Promotion
Stone#3: Branding
Stone#4: Omnipresence
Stone#5: Teamwork

Stone#1 (Product) – Product is a given. It's the product or service you provide to the consumer. Stones #2 - #3 are the means by which you sling stone #1. Stones #4 - #5 are how you kill the Goliath of obscurity. Without stones #2 - #5 you will never kill the Goliath.

Stone#2 (Marketing & Promotion)

Marketing – The action or business of promoting and selling products or services, including market research and advertising.

Promotion – To further the progress of something, especially a cause, venture, or aim; support or actively encourage.

What was David Marketing & Promoting?

By faith in God, he was marketing victory. *"We can defeat this uncircumcised Philistine!"* By one courageous act, he promoted freedom. *"This day the Lord will deliver you into my hand, and I will strike you and take your head from you."*

Stone#3 (Branding)

Branding - According to Entrepreneur Magazine, *Branding* is the marketing practice of creating a name, symbol or design that identifies and differentiates a product from other products.

What was David Branding?

While the armies of Israel branded themselves as cowards, afraid to fight Goliath, David branded himself as courageous, fully relying on God. Not one ounce of doubt could be found in him. He even refused King Saul's armor.

Stone#4 (Omnipresence)

Omnipresence – Present everywhere at the same time. Widely or constantly encountered; common or widespread.

How was David Omnipresent?

David went on to fight and win many battles across the land. Everywhere he marched, he was victorious. He was persistent and consistent. Everyone everywhere knew David as a mighty man of God who would conquer and destroy any enemy who dared tempt the God of Jacob.

Stone#5 (Teamwork)

Teamwork –The combined action of a group of people, especially when effective and efficient.

How did David engage in Teamwork?

The day David killed Goliath, he ran down the mountain into the valley with his sling and took Goliath out before he even knew he had been hit! It only took one stone to kill the giant, but David had four more. Many believe it was because David was prepared incase Goliath's four brothers showed up to challenge him. However, once David took out Goliath, the Philistine soldiers began to flee. Then, the Israelite army pursued them, killing all they could find. By no stretch of the imagination, would the young boy David have been capable of chasing and killing the Philistine army with only four stones, but because of teamwork, he didn't have too!

So, now that we've gone over the Four Forgotten Stones of business, have you figured out what David's product was?

What was David's Product?

King Saul had lost favor with God, and so God was positioning David to reign as King, moving him from the field to the palace. David would soon take over the throne. Like all great leaders, David showed confidence, faith, courage, strength, and trust in God. David became King in 1010 BC. Who would have thought that we could learn so much about growing a business from a Bible story we read to our children before bedtime? If you follow the business model of David, I truly believe that you will position yourself to reign in the market place. David himself, was the product!

"Success is only in the sling of the one willing to aim high enough."
~Nate Fortner

CHAPTER 24

The Making of a #1 Best Seller

Have you ever wondered how to make your book a #1 Best Seller? The answer is simple, but the process you choose to make it happen may not be so simple. The answer to making any book a #1 Best Seller is to have books flying off of the shelves. Sounds easy enough don't you think? You must be getting a ton of attention. You need to make sure your book is getting distribution, and then, people must know your book exists. Distribution will never be enough.

Writing your book was the easy part. Selling it is the hard part. Make sure to get as much publicity as possible. Learn to become omnipresent, and push for celebrity status in your town. Once you've established yourself as a local celebrity, start expanding your reach. If you ever expect your book to take off and be a success, you must get attention.

Marketing is going to require you to be creative. You must stand out, or at least a head taller than everyone else. You need a mob rushing into bookstores nationwide buying your books when they release. You can read any book on marketing and advertising that you want, but I assure you, they will all tell you the same thing. Your message must constantly be in the sight and mind of your target market.

Go ahead and tear down the walls of doubt, and get committed to success! Marketing and promoting your book is like eating. You have to do it every day if you want to gain energy. Pour your heart into it. There is no marketing miracle cure. There is no secret to selling millions of copies instantaneously. You must live to market, and market to win! "Word of Mouth" will never make you a #1 Best Seller! "Word of Mouth" and "Getting Attention" are almost the same, but they're not. "Word of Mouth" means people are talking about you. "Getting Attention" is putting your message into their face whether they want to see it or not. "Word of Mouth," can also hurt you. It just takes one bad egg to ruin the bunch. Make sure you are creating the buzz you want people to know about your book. You need to push hard every day!

You must sell people on the idea that your book will solve the problems they are currently facing in their lives, whether it be business, religion, relationship, etc. It's time to leave your mark on this planet. Make sure people know who you are, even if it requires you standing on the street with a cardboard sign saying you'll read for $1.00. You must make a commitment to live a life dedicated to making sure your book sits on every coffee table, is in every doctor's office, is in every hotel room, and every prisoner has read your book. You want people chanting your name in the streets and from the roof tops. You must be purpose driven!

"May the Lord give you the desire of your heart and make all your plans succeed." (*NKJV*, Psalm 20:3)

CHAPTER 25

Videos Gone Wild (Viral)

If you aren't creating video content, you are already losing valuable followers. We all know followers eventually convert to buyers, if we nurture these contacts. Great videos can go viral! Place a call to action in your video to buy a product, visit a website, or something. There are a few of our current celebrities like Justin Bieber to mention one, who have found success through video. Don't discredit video! Make your content go viral using YouTube.com or Vimeo.com.

Video Optimization

1. Keywords – Use the Google keywords tool. www.Google.com/keywords
2. Content – Produce High Quality Valuable Content – Fresh & Reliable.
3. Community – Get more Subscribers. Grow your realm of influence.
4. Back Links – Encourage others to embed your videos in their websites and blogs.
5. Regularity – Post on a regular scheduled basis instead of dumping a ton of content all at once.

Scan QR Code

Or Type the link below into your web browser
https://www.youtube.com/watch?v=nzRWecw47y8

CHAPTER 26

Don't Disrespect Your Publisher

When I published my first book "Teaching Christians to Pray the Bible Way," I had published with a well-known publisher. It was such an exciting experience and I felt a great sense of accomplishment. I had accomplished at 24 years old, what many only achieve after a lifetime. After just a few short months, I was very unhappy with the results I had gotten. I called my publisher and asked that they remove me from their database as an author. I decided I was going to start my own company and help authors to keep them from going through what I did. Needless to say, I did start my own company, and I've just hit my three year anniversary. I will tell you, I have dealt with some crazy people. One particular author, who I won't name, would constantly text and call my phone harassing me, wanting to know why her book wasn't selling. She would text hateful messages to my phone wanting to know when she would be receiving her royalty check. "I know my book's good, and people will buy it if you'd just promote it like you're supposed to do!" she claimed. Can you guess why she didn't receive a royalty check? The answer is simple! Her book was still in the editing process! The book wasn't even close to being finished yet, and this woman was harassing me and my Editor like crazy. Later, I found out that she had befriended my Editor, and my Editor, out of the kindness of her heart, paid money over the phone to a Drug Store to pay for this woman's prescription medication! My Editor is an amazing woman, but I didn't know she had done this until after the fact. Then the old woman still bit the hand that fed her. What a dog!

Once her book was published, I scheduled her for a couple of book signings here in town, and afterward, the bookstore owners begged me not to bring her back for another event. At one point, this author called my Editor and told her that if I would focus my attention on promoting her book instead of my own and the other authors, she could make some money. Let me just tell you, if this is the attitude you have toward your publisher, be prepared to get dropped! Once I completed her book, I put it out into the market place, and believe it or not, it was starting to pick up momentum. She was even getting some really awesome reviews, and she was excited. I was so happy knowing that maybe now we would work together peaceably. I was so terribly wrong! Just a few days later, my Editor called me, and I could tell by the tone of her voice that she was not very happy! This author had begun texting and harassing her again. Now, it had just went too far, because stores around town were calling and asking if I was still representing her. She had started going to stores around town slandering me and my company.

The moral of the story is NEVER publicly harass your publisher simply because he/she isn't moving as fast as you think he/she should. This work typically takes 18 months, and we do it in 8. We work very hard to make our authors look great! I ended up dropping her, and cut all ties. She was too much to handle. What makes this even worse, is I never even charged this ungrateful woman the first dollar. I invested $1,500.00 of my own money into her book! I believe in helping people, and this woman simply had no money, but my Editor believed so strongly that her book would become a Best Seller. This woman was such a great writer that my Editor had me so excited to invest my own $1,500.00 into someone else's work.

About a year later, I received a call from another publisher asking if I knew about a very hateful old woman who evidently I had published at some point. I said, "Let me guess, her name was ******* *******?" "Yep, that's her!" he said. She had entered his office slandering me and my company saying how badly we treated her. I told him to stay away from the woman because she's trouble. He told me that he had no intention of publishing her writing simply because she came in speaking so badly of me and my company.

Obviously, I'm sure there may be some bad publishers out there, but I've not met one yet. Make sure before you publish with *any publisher* that you completely understand the contract. All publishers don't offer the same services. Your publisher can't make people buy your book, and your publisher probably won't promote your title. They're also not going to serve as your agent! If you have a poor attitude, you won't get anywhere!

The main point is this!

Don't disrespect your Publisher, we speak among ourselves and you'll never get published!

CHAPTER 27

Without Faith In Yourself....

As a writer, you must believe in yourself! Regardless of what you may think, you are the mitochondria or powerhouse that will engage readers, pushing them to buy your book. Your publisher can't make people buy your book. The publisher will do exactly as his/her title suggests; publish your book! Most publishers will also handle getting your book into distribution and collect your royalties for you. Let me say it again. Your publisher cannot dedicate countless hours and thousands of dollars to just one book. Some publishers will perhaps, but they all won't.

As an author, it is your responsibility and duty to build your platform. No publisher can do that for you. Even if a publisher could build your platform, would you be able to operate and perform on that stage? I'll also say this. It would be completely unfair to the author if the publisher tried to build each author's platform. We aren't as passionate about your topic as you are! Doctors have the passion to heal; lawyers live to promote the law; authors live to write; singers live to sing and publishers publish! If you need help promoting your book, check out: http://thebookpromoter.com

http://BooksGoSocial.com

If you're going to write a book, you won't get rich and famous overnight! Overnight success is achieved by taking large steps over years of hard work. You need to invest in yourself by reading books on promotion and marketing like, **"Success Requires Action"** by Nate Fortner to start. Get a copy of **"How To Be A Successful Writer Overnight."** It is also another title by Nate Fortner that should interest you. Although, this Kindle book may be more for beginners, well-seasoned authors shouldn't count them out. These would be great resources to remember the basics.

DID YOU KNOW?

College Education is now *FREE* worldwide! It's called YouTube! I'm telling you, when I moved to Alabama, I dropped out of college, and I've learned more on YouTube than I ever did sitting in class! If you plan on being a successful writer, it's time to focus and get committed.

I'm Nate Fortner, and I've written more than seven books to date, and I'm also a Country Christian Recording Artist. I travel the country all year long speaking to groups of authors, and performing concerts to thousands. However, right now you're probably thinking, *"I've never heard of you before now."* You're absolutely correct, and if I hadn't taken the initiative to write this book, you might not still know who I am! Most people who attain celebrity status do it over a period of 10-20 years. As depressing as this may be, the important thing to remember is, they never gave up! They may have gotten knocked down, but they got back up! They kept pushing, and now they are celebrities! I won't say who, but I have many celebrity friends who will tell you the same thing. Stay focused, get committed, and do whatever it takes. If you ever plan on making a difference in this world, you better get serious because you only live once! Watch out because Nate Fortner will be a household name in the next 20 years!

I want to share a few of my songs with you!

God Bless!

Scan QR Code

Or Type the link below into your web browser
https://www.youtube.com/watch?v=WFn_Dl0M7g8&ebc
"Why'd You Take Her Away"

Scan QR Code

Or Type the link below into your web browser
https://www.youtube.com/watch?v=eGETjq6oKW0
"Before the Baptist Do"

Scan QR Code

Or Type the link below into your web browser
https://www.youtube.com/watch?v=QX4FLxVKnEl
"Renew Me I Pray"

CHAPTER 28
"NO More Prancing Reindeer on our #RedCup!"

So, I'm sure by now that you've heard all the saga over the Starbucks #RedCup. Howard Shultz, Chairman and CEO of Starbucks recently made the decision to not have holiday references on their cups for the Christmas season. Instead, they would go with a simple #RedCup. Previous holiday cups portrayed images of prancing reindeer, and other winter characters such as snowmen. It has outraged many of their customers to make such claims that "Starbucks hates Christians," or that "Starbucks has banned Christmas." One I even heard was, "Starbucks hates Jesus." Republican presidential candidate Donald Trump even suggested boycotting Starbucks over the cups. Later, a Starbucks representative stated that they offer a Christmas blend that is available in stores around the world.

Even though we live in America, and Christmas is a major part of our culture, I find it funny that people would expect a Jewish-owned company to have Jesus printed on their cups. Did Starbucks ever have literal Christmas images displayed on their cups to begin with? Snowmen aren't symbolic to Christmas. They're a winter fictional character made popular by Jack Rollins and Steve Nelson in the 1950's when they wrote "Frosty the Snowman," and Gene Autry and the Cass Country Boys released it to radio. On the other hand, if you choose not to support the #RedCup, one thing's for sure. Dunkin' Donuts has risen to the occasion stating that they will gladly continue printing holiday cups.

While the country may be in despair over the #RedCup, one thing still holds true here on Sand Mountain. Jamoka's Coffee Company has been proudly serving our community since 2005. Now with three locations: Boaz, Albertville, and Guntersville. Stop in today and get a latte of holiday drink choices, and remember, #ItsJustACup!

I personally think that whoever's idea this was, is a marketing genius. I'd love to see what sales jumped up to just because of this. I see this as marketing dynamite! After I heard about this, I drove thirty minutes just to go buy a Starbucks cup of coffee. Now, I have my very own #RedCup Souvenir!

A book of interest would be: "Success One Cup at a Time" by Howard Shultz, CEO and Chairman of Starbucks.

CHAPTER 29

Coffee Sleeve Marketing

Put a Little Caffeine in Your Advertising Efforts

The average person will take at least 20 to 30 minutes to drink their morning cup of Joe, so why not put your message directly into their hands?

Literally!

Coffee Sleeve Marketing is a great way to provide your customers with information about upcoming sales or to provide a coupon. WhosoeverPress.com in Boaz, AL. is a Publishing Company that I own. Not only do we publish writers, but we provide different services to our community as well. One of those services is to our local coffee shop called Jamoka's Coffee Company. We provide them with their coffee sleeves, and we do it totally free.

So, here's how it started! As a Publisher working with mainly low-income or never before published authors, I had to develop creative ways for them to promote their books. I was sitting in Jamoka's Coffee Shop here in Boaz, AL. one day when I noticed their coffee sleeve was thick and had a green leaf on it for some reason. I couldn't for the life of me figure out why they didn't have their logo on there. In my mind, I thought, *"You guys need to be building your brand."*

I spoke with the owner that day and asked, "If I could provide you with free coffee sleeves with your logo on the front, would you use them?" She immediately agreed. Now, I just had to figure out how I was going to make it happen.

My original thought was to promote my authors' new titles on the back, but quickly became so hot among local businesses that they were calling me wanting to advertise on the back of my sleeves too! Needless to say, Jamoka's Coffee Company has received approximately 30,000 free coffee sleeves this year, saving them some serious cash!

Not only did they start to brand themselves with their logo on every sleeve, but the local economy was boosted as well, by cross-promoting local businesses on their sleeves. Honestly, it's helped to make my bank account "a latte" happier! Coffee Sleeve Marketing is a win-win for everyone involved.

Become a #Coffeepreneur Today! I'm looking to hire Sales Reps all across the United States. Let's make some money together!

Want to advertise your book or business on the back of 1,000 coffee sleeves? Call my office! We're adding new locations very soon! Mention that you read about Coffee Sleeve Marketing in this book, and get your message on the back of 1,000 sleeves for only $150.00! Regular price is $250.00. Using this book just now right here has already made you $100.00 richer! Well worth the $20.00 investment you paid for this book!

I have an entire training system setup and in place to help you start making money in your town. All you have to do is call my office at 256-706-3315.

Scan QR Code

Or Type the link below into your web browser
https://www.youtube.com/watch?v=tpe5GTz-BPg

Scan QR Code

Or Type the link below into your web browser
https://www.youtube.com/watch?v=vPc47COkvec

Scan QR Code

Or Type the link below into your web browser
https://www.youtube.com/watch?v=c_EdT7f7t7k

Scan QR Code

Or Type the link below into your web browser
https://www.youtube.com/watch?v=J56oD5dpOgU

CHAPTER 30

Recording Radio Interviews

So, you've landed a radio interview? Well, congratulations on your achievement. I'm sure you worked hard to get the interview. I just need to tell you a few things that will help you in the future.

Be sure when you go in to the station, you ask if they will be recording the interview. If so, you want a copy burned on a disc or an email sent to you with the entire interview. Be prepared by taking an audio recorder with you just in case. Be sure to ask permission to record the interview though. I've never been told that I wasn't allowed to record the interview, so try. The really awesome thing is, most cell phones now have built in recorders.

You want a copy of the interview to place on your website. Put this audio into a YouTube video as well. You need this interview, so you can start getting it circulating around the internet. This is another piece of content you can use to help people discover you!

Radio interviews give you credibility. Being heard on radio by family and friends also gives you the local celebrity status. You become a local celebrity, and then build on that. Again, make sure that you obtain a copy of the interview from the station, or record it on your phone. You could also take the audio and upload it as a podcast on your website or iTunes. There is also a free website called www.SoundCloud.com that is popular among Musicians to share their songs, but I use the site to upload and host my Podcasts. This site even allows you the option to embed the audio podcast onto your website! Other companies are charging for this service, so take advantage of free! I convert most of my YouTube videos to mp3 files and upload to SoundCloud.com for my followers to enjoy in their cars. This is yet, another great way of creating and distributing content about your business. Remember, you must think in terms of global proportions. You must become Omnipresent! A radio interview will instantly give you credibility as a reliable resource. Make sure you are scheduling interviews as often as possible, so you can continue to reach new people.

Another great tool is a phone call recorder that you can download for free in the App Store. When you get ready for an interview, turn your phone call recorder on. The quality is great. The one I personally use is called "Automatic Call Recorder." Remember, you need someone's permission before you can record them. Make sure you state that you will be recording the audio for marketing and promotional purposes in the future.

Want to be a guest on my show The Author Minute? Call my office at: 256-706-3315. The interview is recorded, and then converted to a YouTube video that you can start throwing out all over the internet. What will this cost you? Absolutely nothing, but the time it takes to call my office! Oh, and maybe a quarter for the call. Lol.

Here's another tip! Don't look over your local radio stations. Many of them are always looking for new people to interview. Need a comprehensive list of Radio Stations to call? Google it!

"Dreams just don't come true, they are the product of a ton of hard work and dedication to achieve what others have already given up on."

~Nate Fortner

Scan QR Code

Or Type the link below into your web browser
https://www.youtube.com/watch?v=tWwId3YALxU

CHAPTER 31

Top 3 Free Marketing Avenues for Authors

As a Publisher, I constantly have authors asking how they can better promote their books. I honestly wish there was a miracle answer, but there's not. However, I do have three avenues of marketing that I want to discuss with you. I recently spoke with a business owner who is currently worth about $900,000,000. I asked, **"What is the #1 thing that you've done in business that has helped you to get the most massive amounts of attention?"** "His answer was, "Definitely learning to hammer every social media platform." You're probably thinking you don't have time to be on all these social media platforms and run your business, right? The truth is, if you want massive attention, you need to provide massive amounts of content!

The top 3 Free Marketing Avenues Are:

1. Blogs
2. Video
3. Social Media

Blog Marketing

What is a blog?

A blog is a website or web page that is updated by an individual or small group that post articles on a specific topic.

We all know that Google loves fresh quality content. Right now, some of my previous blog posts are showing up on the first page of Google search results. This is where you need your content being displayed. When you can provide quality content on a regular basis, you become a valuable source of information. Be sure that you're providing solutions to problems in your blog posts. Honestly, no one cares what color your shoes are. They want to know where they can buy a pair for themselves.

Quality Content - hinges on the truth. Don't spread false information, or you could be blacklisted by those who just read your article. Then, guess whose article will be passed over next time they search for content? Content is king!

Frequency - Develop a schedule for when your articles will post on your blog and be consistent. Posting once a month will never produce the results you're searching for in return. At first, I know it can be daunting for some to constantly be coming up with new content, but keep brainstorming for topics. The more you post, the more Google will have to work with, ultimately helping you to be discovered. I would suggest posting at least once a week. If you're ready to roll, post once or twice per week. One of my authors, Christy Smith, Author of "Forever and Always" is a Historical Romance author. I understand, she can only post so much about her novella, but what I suggested to her was to start writing either historical or romance articles. Writing like this, she will never run out of material, and she could always find a creative twist to add a plug for her book.

Keywords - Figure out what the main topics are in your article. Those words or phrases are your keywords and key phrases. If you're posting on Blogger.com, these are called labels. This is where we get into SEO, short for Search Engine Optimization. These are the words or phrases that others will be searching for on Google. When you have these words selected as your key words or labels, then guess whose article is going to have a better chance of showing up?

For more ideas on Blogging, visit:

http://HowToMakeMyBlog.com

"Quality content in the hands of your prospect produces sales."

~Nate Fortner

Video Marketing

Videos can find their way into the eyes of your target market if you do it right. Producing great video content can make your content go viral. Of course, when you hear of a video that has gone viral, it's usually something so cool that people just can't seem to get enough of it. Sometimes, viral just happens.

What is viral?

Think in terms of sickness or disease. It can be viral and affect the entire body. For your video to be viral, it needs to be infecting the internet like the plague. Your content needs to be contagious!

The same principles that apply to blogs, also apply to videos.

1. Quality Content
2. Frequency
3. Keywords

You need hundreds of videos going out all over the internet. You should be uploading videos on YouTube, Vimeo, Facebook, LinkedIn, Twitter, and all other social media platforms.

"You need massive attention everywhere, not a massive billboard somewhere."

~Nate Fortner

CHAPTER 32

Social Media Marketing

What is Social Media?

According to Google, *Social Media* is websites and applications that enable users to create and share content or to participate in social networking.

Let's break it down a little more.

What does it mean to be social?

Being social is basically gathering together as a group or organization and communicating with each other. Being social could mean going to church, a party, a club, or any other place where people are gathering to hang out.

What is Media?

According to Google, media is the main means of mass communication (especially television, radio, newspaper, and the internet).

Now, what is social media?

Social Media according to Nate is any place online where people are gathering to share content. This includes pictures, videos, articles written on blogs, or even audio podcasts.

If you plan to be heard, and get the news out about your book, you must learn to use Social Media. Social Media can instantly allow you to travel the world without even leaving your house.

"Success has been written in the stars, only for those willing to shoot that high."

~Nate Fortner

Nate Fortner, Author of *"Book Marketing in the 21st Century,"* and *"How To Be a Successful Writer Overnight."*

Scan QR Code

Or Type the link below into your web browser
https://www.youtube.com/watch?v=JX5qR_YhVj4

CHAPTER 33

26 Social Media Platforms You Should Be Using

4. Facebook
5. Twitter
6. LinkedIn
7. YouTube
8. Vimeo
9. Pinterest
10. Instagram
11. Blogger
12. Google Plus
13. Heaven Up
14. Tumblr
15. VK
16. Flickr
17. Vine
18. Meetup
19. Tagged
20. Ask.fm
21. Meetme
22. Classmates
23. Xing
24. Renten
25. Snapchat
26. Twoo

27. Yelp.com- Although this isn't necessarily a social platform, there are currently 139 million active users and 67 million reviews according to inboundboulder.com
28. Reddit
29. Swarm

CHAPTER 34

How Do I Get An ISBN For My Book?

ISBN stands for The International Standard Book Number. It's a 13-digit number that identifies your book and publisher. If you're going to be selling your book through a distribution chain, then you need an ISBN. If you're just going to hand it out to your family and friends, then don't waste your money purchasing an ISBN.

To purchase an ISBN, visit www.MyIdentifiers.com. The cost for a single ISBN is $125.00 or you may purchase a block of ten for $295.00. If you're a large Publishing House, then you may want to purchase a block of 1,000 ISBN's for a rate of only $1.00 each.

You will also need a barcode for your book, which is a separate cost of $25.00. The barcode can also be purchased from the myidentifiers.com website. The bar code is what stores use to scan the book at the time of purchase. It's important to note that if you're publishing with a well-established publishing house, then they will purchase the ISBN and bar code for you.

CHAPTER 35

How Do I Purchase a Library of Congress Number for My Book?

Obtaining an LOC# for your book is quite easy. The LOC# is issued prior to publication, and is for books intended for distribution to libraries. It's called the Preassigned Control Number (PCN) and may be requested simply by visiting http://pcn.loc.gov. You will be required to create an account, which is easy. Then, you simply request the LOC# (PCN#) by submitting the one-page application. Typically your number will arrive in your email inbox within ten days, but usually only takes a couple of days. Make sure you or your Publisher places the Library of Congress # on the Copyright page of your book. Once the book is printed, one complimentary copy needs to be mailed to the Library of Congress.

Library of Congress
US Programs, aw, and Literature Division
Cataloging in Publication Program
100 Independence Avenues, S.E.
Washington, DC. 20540-4283

There are no fees for participating in the PCN program. The LOC# is FREE! While all books aren't eligible for the program, you can find out if your book qualifies by visiting the PCN website.

CHAPTER 36

How Can I Turn My Paperback Book Into an Audio Book?

It's obvious we are living in different times than we were twenty years ago. Technology has made advancements beyond what many of our minds can comprehend. It seems to me that soon as I learn to use one piece of technology, something new is created to replace my current program. We are living in an ever-evolving world, and we must learn to adapt if we want to survive.

People are busier now more than ever before in history. The average person reads only one book per year. Who has time to read anyway? By time we get home from work, fight with the kids, and eat supper, it's time for bed. We simply need more time. Don't you agree?

As Authors, if we want people engaging with our content, we must provide it in a way they can use. Times are only going to get busier, and let's face it, you need an audio book! What time I don't have to sit and read a book, I do have 30 minutes on the way to and from work every day to listen to an audio book. That's 60 minutes of my time that I'm trapped in my truck that I could be listening to your content.

If you want people actively reading your material, you must make it available on a platform they can use in the midst of their busy schedule. By creating an audio book, you just helped someone create more time in their day to drown themselves in your content.

Want to create your very own audio book?

Visit www.ACX.com

Your book will be made available on Amazon.com, iTunes, and the big one is Audible.com. This is an Amazon.com owned company, so you can rest assured it's a great platform.

Nate Fortner, Author of *"Book Marketing in the 21st Century,"* and *"How To Be A Successful Writer Overnight."*

CHAPTER 37

Why All the Crappy Books?

So many of the marketing and advertising books I've read, all teach the same techniques. Why is it that people think they can keep recycling garbage that doesn't work? Out of all the books in the world, where are all the good ones? When I read a book, I want quality information that I can apply to my life, my situation, or day right then. I want a book that provides me with websites, phone numbers, emails, addresses and strategies.

I've got two books that I'd like to recommend that have changed my life. The first is "Free Marketing," 101 Low and No-Cost ways to Grow Your Business Online and Off by Jim Cockrum. This book made me feel like a kid in a candy store. Every turn of the page, I was learning something new. Each chapter provided me with valuable websites, stats, and people to contact, etc. It was the perfect book. I contribute much of my business success over the past three years to "Free Marketing." http://JimCockrum.com

The second book I'd like to recommend is "The 10X Rule" by New York Times Bestselling Author, international sales expert, sales trainer, and motivational speaker, Grant Cardone. As the cover states, "The only difference between success and failure," is the 10X Rule. I came across Grant Cardone for the first time in December of 2014, while searching for Zig Ziglar videos on YouTube.

At first, I was turned off by Grant's foul language in his videos. I couldn't believe this guy had such intelligence and yet had such a poor vocabulary. While I was turned off by his foul language, I was very quickly excited by his wisdom. The guy was just spewing knowledge all over my computer screen. For the next few weeks, I ate, drank, watched, listened, and devoured any and all content by Grant Cardone. I was visiting my family in the mountains of West Virginia that Christmas, and I knew I had to have more of Grant Cardone. I went straight to the mall to purchase his book, "The 10X Rule."

Needless to say, Grant Cardone has been a huge business inspiration to me this year. I've doubled my income this year since I started following Grant online. This upcoming year, my company will more than double its income because of the teachings of Grant Cardone.
http://GrantCardone.com

CHAPTER 38

How Can People Subscribe to my Blog on Blogger.com?

I've been searching for a while now, how to allow people to be able to subscribe to my blog posts on Blogger.com. I eventually came to the conclusion that it wasn't going to happen until I discovered a trick using a free email marketing service called mailChimp.com Check out the video below and get your mind blown as you see for the first time how people can subscribe to your blog on Blogger.com.

Scan QR Code

**Or Type the link below into your web browser
https://www.youtube.com/watch?v=s6NFXcFAkT8**

CHAPTER 39

3 Killer Tips to growing a Successful Business

Like all great businesses, they are developed over a period of time and built on the base of a well thought out marketing plan. Success isn't free, and it certainly isn't easy. When developing a marketing plan, you must understand that you are growing a brand, not just a company.

Tip#1: Commitment- *"Till death do we part!"* is what true commitment looks like. This line is recited by happy couples throughout the world every day! Through the good, the bad, and the ugly, you must be committed to success. There will be times in your business that you will want to shut the doors and quit. You will probably get depressed from time to time, but real results will only come when you get committed. You must make up in your mind and spirit that failure is not an option for you!

Understanding the Difference between Investing and the Means by Which We Do So

Tip#2: Investment- *"Relentlessly pursuing more!"* Recently, I asked on Social Media, *"What do you consider to be your greatest investment?"* Of course, everyone had an answer. Some said God, some said their kids, or even their careers. As much as I liked their answers, they were all wrong. God, kids, careers, etc; could indeed be an investment to some degree, but they are not your greatest investment. God, kids, and careers are the means by which we invest!

For Example: Say you want to grow in your relationship with God, what do you do? You obviously invest into the relationship, but how? Your greatest investment isn't God; it's your relationship with God that you invest in by reading the Bible, praying and going to church, etc.

Here's another example: Say you want to be a millionaire. How do you become a millionaire? Well, I know one thing. You don't get money by simply believing that it's going to show up. Not one time has the gas tank on my truck filled up miraculously without me paying for fuel. You don't invest in a millionaire to become a millionaire. You don't invest in fuel to fill your gas tank. Do you understand where I'm going with this yet?

Let's talk about your kids for a minute. Your kids are probably the most awesome benefit of your investments. Yes, you can invest in your kids, but hold on a second. Just hear me out. Your young children under the age of eighteen and sometimes even over the age of eighteen aren't capable of surviving without your continued guidance. They need money, clothes, and rides to school or to ball games. Yes, you are investing time into your children, but just hold up another second here. Without you being capable of providing for your children, someone else would be taking care of your kids. Your children are great to invest in, and you need to be investing in your children, but they are not your greatest investment. Have you figured it out yet?

What's your greatest investment? Is it your health? You're getting there, but not quite yet, so here it is: The greatest investment you will ever make is in yourself! YES! YES! YES! You will always be your greatest investment! Everything in your life that you hold dear, is a direct result of an investment.

Your pay check is the result of you investing your time and energy into a job that produces an income for you and your family. You use that money to buy groceries to feed you and your family in order to survive. You buy healthy foods to eat as an investment in your health. You invest money and time into a gym membership to invest in your overall health. You have to understand that all these investments are great, but not possible if you're dead. These are all means by which you protect your greatest investment. YOU!

To sum it all up real quick, your eternal Salvation should be the #1 means by which you invest in yourself. Get to know God. I could quote Bible verses all day long telling you why you need Jesus. Without investing in yourself first, you will never be able to invest in others. Since we are talking business here, you must focus on not only your personal health, but the health of your company. Your company is the investment, but marketing is the means by which you invest.

Tip#3: Consistent- *"No one knows you!"* I've already stated many times that your biggest obstacle in business will be obscurity. The truth is, not enough people know who you are. People must know you exist, if you expect them to do business with you. They need to be seeing you everywhere. Consistency will cause people to become familiar with your company's brand and message. As people become more familiar with you, they will begin to trust you, and trust will eventually lead to a sale. Obviously, this is considering that you are providing a quality product or service.

Do you feel it would be better to have two 60 second TV commercials air each week for two months, or thirty-two 30 second commercials over four months? Bigger isn't always better in small time frames. If money isn't an issue, then by all means, go all out, but be consistent over longer periods of time. You want to capture the largest amount of exposure as possible. If you're on a tight budget, go smaller for longer.

When making cold calls, consistency is also important. Make calls every day. Don't expect 30 or 40 calls once a week to pay the bills. Consistency over longer periods of time will produce greater results. When I get started on the phone each day, I may get 50 calls that no one answers, but I always leave a message. They may never call me back, but they at least were made familiar with my name. Next time I call to follow up, they may answer and recognize my name. They probably won't remember where they heard my name at, but at least they will be familiar with my name.

I have been following these three tips in my own business, and I've seen great success! Of the 168 hours in the week, I spend 6 hours per day making phone calls. I average about 1,250 phone calls between Monday and Friday.

"Massive success requires you to take massive amounts of action."
~ Grant Cardone

Check out: http://GrantCardone.com
Check out: http://Witnation.com

Scan QR Code

Or Type the link below into your web browser
https://www.youtube.com/watch?v=sZizLIAjD2Q

CHAPTER 40

Congratulations!

You are now 75% of the way through this book. How much of this information have you actually started implementing? These strategies will never help you, if you don't apply them!

If you have learned anything from this book so far, I need you to make an investment! I want you to invest in your friends, family, and/or employees. Call my office and order a few copies of this book to distribute to those you care about. If you're concerned about the $20.00 you're going to pay, then you need to stop right now and start over reading from the beginning, because you've completely missed the point of this book.

"Three Killer Tips to Growing a Successful Business" is probably the single greatest chapter in this book. First, you COMMIT! Second, you INVEST! Third, you become CONSISTENT! I'm happy that you committed to making it this far into the book, but now it's time to invest in others. Success also means leading others who are thirsty to the water to drink. Call my office and order as many or as little as you need. Anyone who orders 25 or more will receive FREE Shipping. This book will change your world if you apply the principles I've been teaching. I know this because it's working for me. If you have learned anything so far from

this book, hop over to Amazon.com and write me a 5 Star Review.

CHAPTER 41

Fascinating Pastoral Tactics That Can Help Your Business Grow!

I realized about a year ago that some of the most successful businessmen are Church Pastors. They are also some of the greatest content creators you will ever meet. Every Sunday morning, Sunday night, Wednesday night, and any special services through the week will require a sermon or at least some type of devotion. That's at least three times per week at a minimum that your Pastor has to produce fresh content to preach. How in the world does a Pastor produce such fresh relevant content from a 2,000 year old book? The answers will blow your mind!

Believe me when I say, your Pastor has the keys you need to develop a successful business. As a Minister of the Gospel myself, I know how much time is required to produce a quality sermon. You read the scripture over and over again until you've grasped the understanding of the text. Then, you have to figure out how it applies to modern day living. Next, you have to deliver the message to your congregation in a way that they can easily understand and apply the principles to their own lives. The Pastor is a powerful persuader.

However, not only does a Pastor create content that applies to modern day life grounded on the base of one book, but he lives what he teaches. The point is, the Pastor delivers quality content, he builds a relationship with his church members, he builds trust, and he gets paid. You may not like this example, but you know I'm right. Your Pastor is a master at business! He resells you on the idea of the Gospel message in his sermon every single week. The Pastor has convinced you that what he preaches is true. This chapter isn't even about whether you believe in God or not. I'm simply proving to you that your Pastor is a master businessman.

Pastoring a church is like growing a business. It requires countless hours of research, planning, building relationships, networking, and expanding your reach in the community. Some of the best business advice I've ever learned, has simply been by imitating the actions of great Pastors. I challenge you this week to start watching the behavior characteristics of your Pastor. Watch some TV Evangelists this week, and observe how they carry themselves. Listen to what they say and how they say it.

You simply cannot ignore the fact that most TV Evangelists are loaded. How did they accumulate so much wealth? No, not every Pastor is dipping into the church funds. Be wise and do some research. Google search some of these preachers. When you do, you'll be surprised to learn that many of them own and operate multi-million dollar companies outside of the church. Even if you don't believe in God or the Bible, investing some time to attend a local mega church for a few months could be very beneficial to achieving success in your business. Let your Pastor mentor you from the pew. See if you can pull the business principles for success from your Pastor's next sermon.

CHAPTER 42

Title Generators

I have to admit, it's taken me years to release my creative juices, and it's only been in the last six months that I really started pumping out quality content. I've been fortunate enough to have some of my articles to show up on the first page of the Google results. I always said that if I ever found a money maker, that I would keep the idea all to myself. I would hoard up all the secrets of success, out of fear that someone else would discover my secret and take my money maker. Recently, I realized how ignorant that was of me to be thinking that way. I now understand that I must share with the world what I've learned so I can be a resource of valuable information. The only problem with this concept, is how do I get it out there to the masses? Well, I'm doing it every day through Social Media, Blogs, YouTube, and writing books.

Once I started producing content at the speed of light, I sometimes found it hard to keep the creative juices flowing. I needed help coming up with catchy titles for my articles and videos. Then, I discovered www.TweakYourBiz.com. You will find a plethora of information on this site worth reading, learning, and applying to your business model. Scroll all the way to the bottom of the Home Page and click on *"Title Generator."* Type any word into the generator bar and click submit. This generator will create hundreds of great titles for your projects. It will also organize the title for you into the following sections:

·Lists - *"Master the Art of Marketing with These 5 Tips"*

·Best - *"50 Best Methods of Marketing Domination"*

·How To - *"How To Get Fabulous Marketing on a Tight Budget"*

·Questions - *"Are You Embarrassed by Your Marketing Skills? Here's what to Do!"*

·Love - *"Fall in Love with Marketing"*

·Sex - *"Sexy Marketing"*

·Celebrities - *"What Donald Trump Can Teach You About Marketing"*

·Secrets - *"The Hidden Mystery Behind Marketing"*

·Snark - *"It's About the Marketing Stupid!"*

·Business - *"Pump Up Your Sales With These Remarkable Marketing Tactics"*

·Motivation - *"You Can Have Your Cake and Eat It Too!"*

·Problem - *"Here's a Quick Way to Solve Your Marketing Problems"*

·The Kitchen Sink- *"Warning: Marketing!"*

You can even print or download your results for later use. I use this site constantly. I have articles and videos written and scheduled right now for the next few months. This site has even given me fresh ideas for more articles and videos to create.

CHAPTER 43

Telemarketing Made Easy

Ever wonder how telemarketers get your phone number? Maybe you repeatedly get advertisements in the mail for products you recently researched or purchased. Have you ever asked yourself, *"What if I could get access to some great phone numbers to reach my target market?"* Well now you can, and it's from a reliable source.

InfoUSA.com is your one-stop shop for all the leads you could possibly need. According to their website, the Info USA databases are built from over 4,000 phone directories and over 350 new business sources, including new business filings, daily utility connections, County court houses and public record notices. On their site, they state:

"We gather consumer information from over 100 sources including real estate records, tax assessments, voter registration files, utility connects, bill processors, behavioral data, and more."

Also, it's important to note that InfoUSA verifies by phone every contact to ensure its accuracy. It's also important to mention that InfoUSA has been providing over 40 years of great consumer experience.

Email marketing, direct mail, and targeted mail marketing are all great avenues for getting your information out to the consumer.

"Success requires visibility, and you're not even on the radar."

~Nate Fortner

CHAPTER 44

Storms in the Night

Let's face it, every business will face obstacles at some point along the way. Whether it be a disgruntled employee, low sales, or bad management. As the business owner, you are your company's Strong Tower! You are the Way Maker! When the waves of uncertainty are raging your way, brace the ship for a crash landing. Your business may be a ship that is sinking. Perhaps, you've already crashed and sank, but marketing can be a life preserver!

It can most definitely be a stressful situation if your business is facing a storm. In this section, I'm going to give you 3 strategy plans to help you in your time of business despair.

#1: *"Cut the Anchors Loose"* – Brief your employees on the problem, and make sure each one is pulling their own weight. Cut loose any anchors (employees) that are holding you company back from success. Each employee needs to be operating at peak capacity. Make all low performing employees walk the plank before everyone is forced to abandon ship as you go down at the bow.

#2: *"All Hands on Deck"* – When a ship is taking on water, everyone needs to start scooping. Each person on your sales team needs to be 10Xing their work load to be producing massive results. As Grant Cardone says, *"Average is a failing formula."*

#3: *"Docking in the Harbor"* – As the harbor is a shelter or place of safety for a ship, your business must find its harbor. You need to be producing so much success that if you have a bad month or face a storm, you can rest in the harbor. Before you go one more nautical mile, you must realize that abandoning ship is not an option. You must maneuver quickly to keep from crashing.

"Let the winds of success fill your sails, navigating you toward domination."

~Nate Fortner

CHAPTER 45

The Locked Door of Soliciting

When there's a sign on the door that *reads "Absolutely No Soliciting!"* that's just stupid! I recently drove to a few local businesses introducing myself and my coffee sleeve business. One of the businesses had a humongous sign on the front door stating *"Absolutely No Soliciting!"* I thought to myself, *"How Stupid!"* Obviously they're afraid they won't be able to control their buying habits.

As a business owner, I want people trying to get my attention. I need to know about products and services that will help me run my company more efficiently. When I see a *"No Soliciting"* sign on a door or window, I get excited because I know I'm about to start building a new relationship. I go in and ask to speak with the owner or manager if the owner isn't available. I position myself to get attention. I'm either going to have an easy sale or I'll be asked to leave. Either way, I'll follow up at least 10 more times, whether it be by phone, postcard, certified letter, or whatever I have to do to get their attention. Any company that hangs a sign saying *"No Soliciting!"* is begging to be sold to by me. Again, they're usually the easy ones. Hard at first, but always easy after that!

The fact is, you have a product or service that you know will help that business owner to more efficiently run his company. Don't give up until he bites and you reel him in like a fish.

"The best success in life is achieved by helping others achieve success in their lives." ~Nate Fortner

CHAPTER 46

The Invisible Streams

For a business to be successful, you need to be making a profit. Profit keeps the lights on. Profit puts fuel in the car. Profit assures you and your family won't go hungry. When growing your business, you must create multiple streams of income. One of my companies pays me a large sum usually five or six times a year, but it's not enough to live on for the whole year. Another stream of income I have pays me around $250.00 15 to 20 times per year. Another stream of my company pays me very small amounts 50-100 times per year. I wouldn't be able to survive without these multiple streams of income.

For example, one of my streams is provided by the coffee industry. My company provides coffee sleeves to churches and coffee shops across the country. Every single month, I know I have a certain amount of money coming. You need to make sure that you have at least one steady stream that is producing enough profit to cover your monthly expenses. You don't want to be stressed wondering if your bills are going to get paid or not. Once you have one stream established and producing a profit, move on to another.

Creating an additional stream of income is not as hard as you may think. Look at your current product or service, and figure out how it could create more income for you. For example, I was providing coffee sleeves to my local coffee shop by selling ads on the back of the sleeves. I already had the coffee sleeve business established, so then, I created another stream of income by selling coffee sleeves to churches with their church names printed on them. Now, I have churches mailing me checks each month. Develop a plan that works along-side your current business model, and create a new stream of income for your company.

"It only takes one stone of effort to create ripples in the waters of success."

~Nate Fortner

CHAPTER 47

You Need a Comprehensive Bookstore Contact List

As an author, you need people reading your books. Your Publisher has already done the work of getting you into distribution, so bookstores have access to your book. It's up to you to contact them and get them to order your book. You need to be promoting your book so much that readers are going into their local bookstores asking for your book. This will help create interest for bookstore owners to start keeping your books in stock on their shelves. You may even try in your marketing campaigns to push people to their local bookstores to buy your book instead of pushing them to purchase from online stores. If you have no money to purchase a list of Bookstores from InfoUSA.com, start Googling bookstores in your state. Once, you've hit up every bookstore in your state, start branching out.

CHAPTER 48

I Need a Vacation!

Success isn't defined by how much time you visit family, or how long you stay on vacation. Success isn't even measured by your production level. Success is measured by producing results! Are you producing sales in your business? Are you moving inventory? As an author, your book is your business, and you need to treat it as a business! Just because you write a book, doesn't mean it's going to sell.

"Success doesn't happen by accident, it's purposely created!"

~Nate Fortner

CHAPTER 49

Dangerous Marketing

It is a dangerous challenge to put everything on the line for an opportunity to share your book with the next person. When statistics show that the average author sells less than 500 copies of their book in a lifetime, you have to ask some serious questions!

1. Why are you playing the role of an Author?
2. Are you writing out of passion, or simply trying to make a quick dollar? There is no real money in writing books in the short term.
3. If your book ceased to exist, would anyone notice? You've put your heart and soul into your book, so obviously your friends and family would probably notice. The real question is, would the world notice if your book ceased to exist?
4. Will you commit to winning? Vince Lombardi once said, *"Winning isn't everything, it's the only thing!"* Winners have a high level of passion. They stay focused on success, and they're willing to sacrifice to win. You must remember, you're not competing with other authors. Your book needs to be so popular that your book dominates the market in your genre. It's time for authors to start pushing and marketing like crazy!
5. Who is building your brand? While your Publisher cannot build your platform, they can help you to start building your brand through marketing. Building your brand is done by utilizing many different avenues such as TV, Radio, Blogging, Newspapers, etc.

Dangerous Marketing doesn't mean to become entangled in dangerous activities. It simply means that you need to get so seriously committed to having the 7 Billion people on the planet know who you are, so they'll buy your book!

CHAPTER 50

Persistence Isn't Pestering, It's Educating!

Doubt will bring about death to any entrepreneur. Have you ever walked into a room and felt the tension in the air? Atmosphere can determine if a sale is made or not made. Be aware that your prospect can sense your attitude as well. Let me just say, your business will never succeed if you don't believe in your product! If you wouldn't use the product you're selling, then how can you expect others to buy your product? If you doubt your product, the prospect will sense your lack of faith. Your doubt will eventually manifest as the death of your book.

You must believe 100% that your product is the answer to the world's problems! You must be sold on your book. What is it that makes you believe in your product so much? Is it really that good? You may have the greatest product on the market, but you must be willing to educate the community on the need for your product. Not everyone is going to accept your product right off the bat. There will be skeptics and doubters, but you must make them believe by demonstration and persistence. Follow up with a doubting prospect is an absolute must! Most sales will never take place on the first interaction. Follow up until they buy!

Persistence proves you believe in your product. Persistence isn't pestering, it's educating the ignorant. Ignorant doesn't mean the stupid, it means the uninformed or uneducated. By bringing your product to the market place, you are presenting an answer to a problem. Look, it's a cure to the sick, it's a tool to the mechanic, and it's a pencil to the writer! It's your business! Your book is your business!

Start educating people on your product, and persist until they buy. If people still don't buy from you, drive them crazy with your success. At some point, they'll buy just to get you to leave them alone. Then, you follow up! Most Sales Reps never follow up, and they miss the sale. As an author, your product is your book. There are tons of books published every day around the world. How will yours stand out in the crowd? Focus and get committed to success!

CHAPTER 51

Jesus Was a Business Man

Success requires you to be around people. If you're shy or timid, it's time to get over it. You must go to your target market. Just because you start a business, doesn't mean people will start beating your door down to buy your products. People who make it possible for you to succeed must know you exist!

"You will never possess what you are unwilling to pursue."

~Dr. Mike Murdoch

The best example to mention here is Jesus. Whether you believe in Him as the Son of God or not, it is worth reading the Four Gospels in the Bible, simply to learn His business secrets. Jesus walked everywhere He went, and always managed to get people's attention. He walked all over the country spreading His message. Jesus knew if He wanted His message to spread, He had to get people talking about Him. Here we are 2,000 years later, and people are still speaking of Jesus. Everywhere Jesus went, He provided a solution to each person's need. Jesus knew He would be leaving, and He needed dedicated followers to continue spreading His message after His death. Through the three years of His ministry, Jesus was teaching twelve other men who would continue training others to carry His message to the world. In all Jesus did, He was constantly reaching out to people.

Jesus's message has gone global, and now your message needs to go global as well.

How? Develop a Jesus mentality and start walking! You have to get out there! Start training others how to promote your product, and start pushing them out into the market place. Get in your car and drive door to door. Reach for the phone, or get on the computer. Do something! Success starts with you! Go global with the principles Jesus taught! Jesus was most definitely the greatest business man to ever walk the face of the planet!

CHAPTER 52

You Need a Comprehensive List of Libraries

Where are you spending your advertising dollars? Why not get FREE advertising? You have to get creative, and stop throwing your money everywhere hoping for results. I want to get inside your head, and mess up your way of thinking. When you pay for radio or TV ads, once it's played, it's over. If anyone even seen it or heard it, who knows? Who is your generic market? The answer is readers. Who is your target market? The answer will vary depending upon your niche. First of all, where in any town do most of the books exist? Either at the bookstore or the Local Public Library. What does every Library place inside of every book that is checked out? The answer is a bookmark! This strategy is going to freaking blow you away, I know! Start spending some of your advertising dollars on getting bookmarks printed and ship them free of charge to Public Libraries across the country. The key to this is to make sure the bookmarks are full color and have a promotional advertisement promoting your book! Do you realize how many times a day people could actually have your message physically placed into their hands? This concept is going to blow your marketing and promotion to a whole new level! By doing this, you are creating a solution to a problem. You are providing what the Library needs by giving them free bookmarks. You are saving them money because now they won't have to order as many. Guess what? Not everyone is going to be interested in your book, but some will either check it out during their next visit to the Library, or they'll buy it from their local bookstore. It's time to get creative and start investing your money into advertising that will work for you over and over again. Oh yeah, and if you Want to order bookmarks, call my office at 256-706-3315, and mention that you read about this idea in my book "Success Requires Action" and I'll give you a discount on your first 1,000 bookmarks.

Make sure that before you start shipping bookmarks all over the country, you call the Libraries ahead of time, and ask them if they would be able to accept free bookmarks if you send them. Some Libraries may not be able to accept them for some reason. If they can't use them, then your money just got tossed in file 13! Be creative, but be smart as well.

Visit www.PublicLibraries.com for a full list of Public Libraries across the United States. The list will include the name of the Library, their address, and even their phone number.

You're not paying to advertise, you're paying to print bookmarks, and you're literally sending your advertising dollars into battle!

CHAPTER 53

Vision in the Ashes

Do you have the power of vision? Would you like to have the power of vision? Why do you need vision?

1. Vision brings boldness to promote your product or service.
2. Vision gives you strength and courage to speak up in a crowd.
3. Vision helps you to overcome rejection.

The power of vision will give you the ability to become stronger in business. As an author, your writing is your business, and your book is your product!

Maybe at one point, you were on fire in business, but like a hot coal, you cooled off. Now you just feel like a pile of ashes. Well, I'm going to show you how to get back into the fire, and how you can become a contagious business.

Webster defines Contagious - *something spread by direct or indirect contact.* That means if you touch somebody or even if you simply walk past someone, they can catch what you've got.

How would you like for your business to become so contagious that you infect everyone with your message?

Imagine you walk into the meeting, and people instantly know there's something different about you and your company. The people you walk past say to themselves, *"I've got to buy his/her product!"* It's time for you to infect your world, but you must first get into the fire!

How do you get into the fire?

It's a step of action. You must first commit to increasing knowledge by reading every day. You must have a passion to learn and apply what you learn. You must set your mind on fire with knowledge, and grow in wisdom daily. Your thought process needs to change from a "Whatever Happens" mentality to a "Success Happens Here!" mindset. It's time to take control of your thinking.

Many successful business owners know what it's like to feel like a pile of ashes. They've had it and lost it all multiple times. I've heard Dave Ramsey even say he lost it all, but he's back on top again.

How hot is your vision for success? Maybe you were once on fire with vision, but after a while you just cooled off. Now you think your product is subpar since you fell short in the past. All businesses face some type of failure. We all fall short sometimes, but it's how we get back up that makes us great. Let your vision empower you once again! Tell somebody about your product or service. Get a hold of the vision.

"Success will only rain on those who are under its cloud of dispersement." ~Nate Fortner

Get to the fueling station of VISION!

When you put gold into a fire and melt it, the fire burns out all of the impurities. The fire purifies and gives the gold a polished shine. The fire of vision will burn out any impurities, and give you power to grow your business greater than it's ever been. The power of vison will give you hope and strength to face the day. As the owner of your company, what you do really matters because it positively or negatively impacts the lives of others. If you were to lay 100 matches down flat hanging over the edge of a table, just lighting one would cause the whole 100 matches to catch fire. This is how you want to grow your business!

I want to leave you with this next image in your mind. We've all built a real fire at some point in our lives. Let your mind take you back to a campfire in your childhood. Can you smell the scent of hickory and burnt marshmallows in the air yet? After a while, that fire burned out. It looked like a pile of ashes, but once you grabbed that stick off the ground and started stirring the ashes, you saw those red hot glowing embers. That red hot ember is in you! All you need is a little stir to get the flames reaching to the sky again.

You're getting ready to be a blazing fire that's out of control, and no one will be able to extinguish your flames for success! Get fired up with vision!

"The glowing embers of success will only spark, when your vision is big enough to stir the ashes!"

~Nate Fortner

In Closing

You simply cannot ignore the fact that if you want more success, you have to produce more results. You cannot deny the fact, that to produce more results, you need more people to know you exist. People will never know who you are if you aren't pushing hard every day. You will never attain more money if you can't get sales to increase. Sales produce profits, and profits produce growth. If you're serious about making a difference in the world with your business, you have to commit, invest, be consistent and be persistent! I love the way Grant Cardone says it, *"Money may not make you happy, but not having money won't make you happy either."* Personally, I've been broke all my life, so I know what it's like not to have money. I'd prefer to have millions of dollars in the bank. It's not greed to want more, it's financial security for me and my family's way of life. Even the Bible says that a person who doesn't provide for his family is a loser! Money is not the root of all evil. The love of money is the root of all evil. Having lots of money doesn't make you a sinner, so anyone who tells you that your hunger for more is sinful, is just ignorant to the truth of what the Bible really says.

Success in business requires that you make a profit. I pray that you will begin to take action, and start enjoying a better quality of life.

"Profit is the direct result of relentlessly pursuing success!"

~Nate Fortner

For Media Appearance or Interviews

To schedule an appointment, interview, or other such appearance with Nate Fortner, Please call our office at:

Office: 256-706-3315
Email: Nate@WhosoeverPress.com

Also, visit our website at: www.WhosoeverPress.com

If you're interested in the music ministry of Nate Fortner, then visit: www.NateFortner.com

Resources for Authors

Websites

1. www.TheAuthorZoneLearningCenter.com
2. www.TheWritersLife.com
3. www.WritersDigest.com
4. www.Witnation.com
5. www.GrantCardone.com
6. www.Entrepreneur.com
7. www.Adweek.com
8. www.Bizwomen.com
9. www.ToolKit.com
10. www.BusinessOwnersIdeaCafe.com
11. www.BrandChannel.com
12. www.ChiefMarketer.com
13. www.Womenentrepreneur.com
14. www.Fundability.com
15. www.Mint.com
16. www.PayPal.com
17. www.USChamber.com
18. www.Copyright.gov
19. www.USPTO.gov
20. www.Womma.org
21. www.WritersInCharge.com
22. www.Grammarist.com
23. www.GitomerTV.com
24. www.Buzzsumo.com
25. www.Grammarly.com
26. www.Piktochart.com
27. www.websta.me – Use the Instagram Widget to embed your photos on any website using html code.
28. www.DIYMarketers.com
29. www.WhosoeverPress.com

Books to Read

1. Success Requires Action by Nate Fortner Buy a copy for the Entrepreneurial Author/Business owner in your life.
2. The 10X Rule by Grant Cardone
3. Sell or Be Sold by Grant Cardone
4. Guerilla Marketing by Jay Conrad Levison
5. Think and Grow Rich by Napolean Hill
6. Pour Your Heart Into It by Howard Shultz
7. Free Marketing by Jim Cockrum
8. Business at the Speed of Thought by Bill Gates
9. The Millionaire Next Door by Thomas J. Stanley & William D. Danko
10. Rich Dad, Poor Dad by Robert Kiyosaki
11. Sales Bible- The Ultimate Sales Resource by Jeffrey Gitomer
12. Talent is Never Enough by John C. Maxwell

Downloads

Available at: www.TidyForms.com

1. Employment Application
2. Business Plan Sample
3. Marketing Plan Sample

Subscribe, Follow, and LIKE

1. www.YouTube.com/WhosoeverPress
2. www.Twitter.com/WhosoeverPress
3. www.Facebook.com/WhosoeverPress

Shhhh......Listen!

Do You Hear the Sound of Success?

Here Is Our Entire Sales Catalog!

I'm really trying to make this as easy as possible for you to grow your business by placing this catalog in here for you!

Business Cards- Full Color Front & Back

Standard 2"x3.5" Full Color both sides High Gloss UV Laminate Protection.
Yes, you may order without the UV Laminate Protection. Want rounded edges? $12.00/order.

100	$30.00	.30¢ each
250	$34.98	.14¢ each
500	$35.00	.07¢ each
1000	$58.00	5.8¢ each
2500	$125.00	5.0¢ each
5000	$185.00	3.7¢ each
10,000	$360.00	3.6¢ each
20,000	$600.00	3.0¢ each
30,000	$780.00	2.6¢ each
40,000	$1,000.00	2.5¢ each
50,000	$1,200.00	2.4¢ each
60,000	$1,380.00	2.3¢ each
70,000	$1,540.00	2.2¢ each
80,000	$1,680.00	2.1¢ each
100,000	$2,000.00	2.0¢ each

Business Cards-Full Color Front, No Back
Standard 2"x3.5" Full Color Front, No Back High Gloss UV Laminate Protection on front. No UV on back.

100	$30.00	.30¢ each
250	$34.98	.14¢ each
500	$35.00	.07¢ each
1000	$58.00	5.8¢ each
2500	$125.00	5.0¢ each
5000	$185.00	3.7¢ each

10,000	$360.00	3.6¢ each
20,000	$600.00	3.0¢ each
30,000	$780.00	2.6¢ each
40,000	$1,000.00	2.5¢ each
50,000	$1,200.00	2.4¢ each
60,000	$1,380.00	2.3¢ each
70,000	$1,540.00	2.2¢ each
80,000	$1,680.00	2.1¢ each
100,000	$2,000.00	2.0¢ each

Business Cards-Full Color Front, Black & White Back
Standard 2"x3.5" Full Color Front, Black &White Back

100	$30.00	.30¢ each
250	$34.98	.14¢ each
500	$35.00	.07¢ each
1000	$58.00	5.8¢ each
2500	$125.00	5.0¢ each
5000	$185.00	3.7¢ each
10,000	$360.00	3.6¢ each
20,000	$600.00	3.0¢ each
30,000	$780.00	2.6¢ each
40,000	$1,000.00	2.5¢ each
50,000	$1,200.00	2.4¢ each
60,000	$1,380.00	2.3¢ each
70,000	$1,540.00	2.2¢ each
80,000	$1,680.00	2.1¢ each
100,000	$2,000.00	2.0¢ each

Bookmarks
Bookmarks 1.5"X7" OR 2"X8" Color Front, No Back
For 14pt. Gloss Coated Cover, UV Coating will be applied to the color sides, unless **No UV Coating on Back** is selected. If you select Color Front/No Back or Color Front/B&W Back, only the color side (front) will be coated.

100	$60.00	.60¢ each
250	$125.00	.50¢ each
500	$225.00	.45¢ each
1,000	$400.00	.40¢ each
2,500	$875.00	.35¢ each
5,000	$1,500.00	.30¢ each
10,000	$2,500.00	.25¢ each
15,000	$3,000.00	.20¢ each
20,000	$3,600.00	.18¢ each
25,000	$4,000.00	.16¢ each
30,000	$4,200.00	.14¢ each
35,000	$4,550.00	.13¢ each
40,000	$4,800.00	.12¢ each
45,000	$4,950.00	.11¢ each
50,000 – 75,000		.10¢ each
80,000 – 90,000		.07¢ each
100,000	$6,000.00	$0.06¢ each

100,000 + Call Office 26-706-3315

Bookmarks 1.5"X7" OR 2"X8" Color Front, Black & White Back
For 14pt. Gloss Coated Cover, UV Coating will be applied to the color sides, unless *No UV Coating on Back* is selected. If you select Color Front/No Back or Color Front/B&W Back, only the color side (front) will be coated.

100	$60.00	.60¢ each
250	$125.00	.50¢ each
500	$225.00	.45¢ each
1,000	$400.00	.40¢ each
2,500	$875.00	.35¢ each
5,000	$1,500.00	.30¢ each
10,000	$2,500.00	.25¢ each
15,000	$3,000.00	.20¢ each
20,000	$3,600.00	.18¢ each
25,000	$4,000.00	.16¢ each
30,000	$4,200.00	.14¢ each
35,000	$4,550.00	.13¢ each
40,000	$4,800.00	.12¢ each
45,000	$4,950.00	.11¢ each
50,000 – 75,000		.10¢ each
80,000 – 90,000		.07¢ each
100,000	$6,000.00	$.06¢ each
200,000	$10,000.00	$.05¢ each
300,000	$12,000.00	$.04¢ each

Bookmarks 1.5"X7" OR 2"X8" Color Front & Back

For 14pt. Gloss Coated Cover, UV Coating will be applied to the color sides, unless *No UV Coating on Back* is selected. If you select Color Front/No Back or Color Front/B&W Back, only the color side (front) will be coated.

100	$60.00	.60¢ each
250	$125.00	.50¢ each
500	$225.00	.45¢ each
1,000	$400.00	.40¢ each
2,500	$875.00	.35¢ each
5,000	$1,500.00	.30¢ each
10,000	$2,500.00	.25¢ each
15,000	$3,000.00	.20¢ each
20,000	$3,600.00	.18¢ each
25,000	$4,000.00	.16¢ each
30,000	$4,200.00	.14¢ each
35,000	$4,550.00	.13¢ each
40,000	$4,800.00	.12¢ each
45,000	$4,950.00	.11¢ each
50,000 – 75,000		.10¢ each
80,000 – 90,000		.07¢ each
100,000	$6,000.00	$.06¢ each
200,000	$10,000.00	$.05¢ each
300,000	$12,000.00	$.04¢ each

Brochure

8.5"X11" 100lb Gloss Book with Aqueous Coating Tri Fold or Z Fold

100	$120.00	$1.20 each
250	$250.00	$1.00 each
500	$400.00	$.80¢ each
1,000	$420.00	$.42¢ each
2,500	$450.00	$.18¢ each
5,000	$675.00	$.13.5¢ each
10,000	$1,000.00	$.10¢ each

Need Higher Quantities? Call our office at the number provided at the bottom of this page.

Banners

The best way to advertise and promote your business to public. Printed on 15oz premium Scrim Matte and Glossy vinyl. Banners are printed on digital printers using Eco-Solvent inks. The vinyl banners are sturdy and durable with up to 1 year outdoor and 2 years indoor use. Banners are sent out hemmed or taped and grommeted with brass grommets. Full Color. Remember- Most businesses charge $6.00 - $10.00 extra to apply grommets. Ours are included in this price.

2'x4'	$45.00	4'x4'	$60.00
2'x5'	$55.00	4'x5'	$70.00
2'x6'	$65.00	4'x6'	$80.00
2'x7'	$75.00	4'x7'	$90.00
2'x8	$85.00	4'x8'	$100.00
2'x9'	$95.00	4'x9'	$110.00
2'x10'	$105.00	4'x10'	$120.00

3'x4'	$50.00	
3'x5'	$60.00	
3'x6'	$70.00	
3'x7'	$80.00	
3'x8'	$90.00	
3'x9'	$100.00	
3'x10'	$110.00	

Collector's Cards
2.5" X 3.5" with UV Laminate Protection

100	$100.00	$1.00 each
250	$225.00	$.90¢ each
500	$375.00	$.75¢ each
1,000	$500.00	$.50¢ each
2,500	$875.00	$.35¢ each
5,000	$1,250.00	$.25¢ each
10,000	$1,500.00	$.15¢ each
15,000	$1,800.00	$.12¢ each
20,000	$2,000.00	$.10¢ each
25,000	$2,250.00	$.09¢ each

26,000 + Call Office 256-706-3315

Door Hangers
3.5"X8.5" 250 Minimum order
For 14pt. Gloss Coated Cover, UV Coating will be applied to the color sides, unless *No UV Coating on Back* is selected. If you select Color Front/No Back or Color Front/B&W Back, only the color side (front) will be coated. No additional Charge for artwork on back.

250	$212.50	$.85¢ each
500	$375.00	$.75¢ each
1,000	$500.00	$.50¢ each
2,500	$875.00	$.35¢ each
5,000	$1,500.00	$.30¢ each
10,000	$2,000.00	$.20¢ each
15,000	$2,250.00	$.15¢ each
20,000	$2,400.00	$.12¢ each
25,000	$2,500.00	$.10¢ each

Door Hangers 4.25"X11" 250 Minimum order
For 14pt. Gloss Coated Cover, UV Coating will be applied to the color sides, unless *No UV Coating on Back* is selected. If you select Color Front/No Back or Color Front/B&W Back, only the color side (front) will be coated. No additional charge for artwork on back.

250	$212.50	$.85¢ each
500	$375.00	$.75¢ each
1,000	$500.00	$.50¢ each

2,500	$875.00	$.35¢ each
5,000	$1,500.00	$.30¢ each
10,000	$2,000.00	$.20¢ each
15,000	$2,250.00	$.15¢ each
20,000	$2,400.00	$.12¢ each
25,000	$2,500.00	$.10¢ each

Door Hangers JUMBO 5.5"X17" 250 Minimum order

For 14pt. Gloss Coated Cover, UV Coating will be applied to the color sides, unless *No UV Coating on Back* is selected. If you select Color Front/No Back or Color Front/B&W Back, only the color side (front) will be coated. No additional charge for artwork on back.

250	$225.00	$.90¢ each
500	$400.00	$.80¢ each
1,000	$550.00	$.55¢ each
2,500	$1,000.00	$.40¢ each
5,000	$1,750.00	$.35¢ each
10,000	$2,500.00	$.25¢ each
15,000	$3,000.00	$.20¢ each
20,000	$3,400.00	$.17¢ each
25,000	$3,750.00	$.15¢ each

DVD Package
Bleed: 250 Minimum Order
For DVD packages, please build your print-ready digital files by adding 0.1" bleed to each dimension (or 0.05" bleed on all four sides). For example, a 7.1875" x 10.75" DVD package with the full bleed should be 7.2875" x 10.85". Please design your files on our templates to ensure proper bleed.

250	$125.00	$.50¢ each
500	$240.00	$.48¢ each
1,000	$450.00	$.45¢ each
2,500	$1,000.00	$.40¢ each
5,000	$1,900.00	$.38¢ each
10,000	$3,600.00	$.36¢ each
15,000	$5,250.00	$.35¢ each
20,000	$6,000.00	$.30¢ each
25,000	$6,250.00	$.25¢ each
40,000	$8,000.00	$.20¢ each
50,000	$8,500.00	$17¢ each

Envelopes
#10 (4.125"x9.5") Standard Full Color

100	$125.00	$1.25 each
250	$225.00	$.90¢ each
500	$300.00	$.60¢ each
1,000	$500.00	$.50¢ each
2,500	$600.00	$.24¢ each
5,000	$1,150.00	$.23¢ each
10,000	$1,500.00	$.15¢ each

15,000	$1,650.00	$.11¢ each
20,000	$2,000.00	$.10¢ each
25,000	$2,250.00	$.09¢ each
30,000	$2,400.00	$.08¢ each
50,000+	$3,500.00	$.07¢ each

Flyers Full Color Front, No Back
8.5"x11" Printed on 100lb Gloss Book with Aqueous Coating

100	$90.00	$.90¢ each
250	$212.50	$.85¢ each
500	$375.00	$.75¢ each
1,000	$500.00	$.50¢ each
2,500	$875.00	$.35¢ each
5,000	$1,250.00	$.25¢ each
10,000	$1,500.00	$.15¢ each
15,000	$1,650.00	$.11¢ each
20,000	$1,800.00	$.09¢ each
25,000	$2,000.00	$.08¢ each
50,000	$3,500.00	$.07¢ each
75.000	$4,875.00	$.065¢ each
100,000	$6,000.00	$.06¢ each

Flyers 8.5"x11" Full Color Front & Back
Printed on 100lb Gloss Book with Aqueous Coating

100	$95.00	$.95¢ each
250	$225.00	$.90¢ each
500	$400.00	$.80¢ each
1,000	$550.00	$.55¢ each
2,500	$1,000.00	$.40¢ each
5,000	$1,500.00	$.30¢ each
10,000	$2,000.00	$.20¢ each
15,000	$2,400.00	$.16¢ each
20,000	$2,800.00	$.14¢ each
25,000	$3,250.00	$.13¢ each
50,000	$6,000.00	$.12¢ each
75.000	$8,250.00	$.11¢ each
100,000	$9,000.00	$.09¢ each

Flyers 11"x17" Full Color Front, No Back
Printed on 100lb Gloss Book with Aqueous Coating

100	$125.00	$1.25 each
250	$250.00	$1.00 each
500	$400.00	$.80¢ each
1,000	$750.00	$.75¢ each
2,500	$900.00	$.36¢ each
5,000	$1,250.00	$.25¢ each
10,000	$2,000.00	$.20¢ each
20,000	$3,000.00	$.15¢ each
30,000	$4,200.00	$.14¢ each
40.000	$5,200.00	$.13¢ each
50,000	$6,000.00	$.12¢ each
60,000	$6,600.00	$.11¢ each
70,000	$7,000.00	$.10¢ each

Flyers 11"x17" Full Color Font & Back
Printed on 100lb Gloss Book with Aqueous Coating

100	$190.00	$1.90 each
250	$375.00	$1.50 each
500	$625.00	$1.25¢ each
1,000	$1,000.00	$1.00¢ each
2,500	$2,250.00	$.90¢ each
5,000	$2,500.00	$.50¢ each
10,000	$3,500.00	$.35¢ each
20,000	$5,000.00	$.25¢ each
30,000	$6,000.00	$.20¢ each
40.000	$6,800.00	$.17¢ each
50,000+	$7,500.00	$.15¢ each

Hang Tags
Hang Tags Color Front, No Back OR Full Color Front & Back
Strings not included. 14pt. Gloss Coated Cover with UV. Color
Front, No Back.

Sizes:		
2"x2"		2"x4"
2"x5.75"		2"x7.5"
2"x2.25"		2"x4.25"
2"x6"		2"x7.75"
2"x2.5"		2"x4.5"
2"x6.25"		2"x8"
2"x2.75"		2"x4.75"
2"x6.5"		2"x3"
2"x5"		2"x6.75"
2"x3.5"		2"x5.25"
2"x7"		2"x3.75"
2"x5.5"		2"x7.25"

100	$75.00	$.75¢ each
250	$175.00	$.70¢ each
500	$325.00	$.65¢ each
1,000	$600.00	$.60¢ each
2,500	$1,375.00	$.55¢ each
5,000	$2,000.00	$.40¢ each
10,000	$3,000.00	$.30¢ each
50,000	$4,000.00	$.08¢ each
100,000	$5,000.00	$.05¢ each

Letterhead
Letterhead Full Color Front, No Back 250 Minimum Order.

250	$225.00	$.90¢ each
500	$375.00	$.75¢ each
1,000	$500.00	$.50¢ each
2,500	$875.00	$.35¢ each
5,000	$1,000.00	$.20¢ each
10,000	$1,200.00	$.12¢ each
15,000	$1,500.00	$.10¢ each
20,000	$1,600.00	$.08¢ each
25,000	$1,750.00	$.07¢ each
100,000	$6,000.00	$.06¢ each

Event Tickets

100lb Gloss Cover with Aqueous Coating Color Front & Back
2"x5.5" with perforation and numbering.

250	$100.00	$0.40 each
500	$185.00	$0.37 each
1,000	$350.00	$0.35 each
2,500	$675.00	$0.27 each
5,000	$1,300.00	$0.26 each
10,000	$2,000.00	$0.20 each

3.5"X8.5" with Perforation and numbering

250	$175.00	$0.70 each
500	$335.00	$0.67 each
1,000	$650.00	$0.65 each
2,500	$1,250.00	$0.50 each
5,000	$1,500.00	$0.30 each
10,000	$2,000.00	$0.20 each

Posters

13"X19" 100lb Gloss Book with Aqueous Coating Color Front,
No Back.

100	$185.00	$1.85 each
250	$350.00	$1.40 each
500	$650.00	$1.30 each
1,000	$1,270.00	$1.27 each
2,500	$2,500.00	$1.00 each
5,000	$3,750.00	$0.75 each
10,000	$5,000.00	$0.50 each

18"X24" 100lb Gloss Book with Aqueous Coating Color Front, No Back.

100	$500.00	$5.00 each
250	$850.00	$3.40 each
500	$950.00	$1.90 each
1,000	$1,000.00	$1.00 each
2,500	$1,750.00	$ 0.70 each
5,000	$3,000.00	$0.60 each
10,000	$5,000.00	$0.50 each

19"X27" 100lb Gloss Book with Aqueous Coating Color Front, No Back.

100	$600.00	$6.00 each
250	$1,000.00	$4.00 each
500	$1,500.00	$3.00 each
1,000	$2,000.00	$2.00 each
2,500	$3,500.00	$1.40 each
5,000	$3,750.00	$0.75 each
10,000	$5,000.00	$0.50 each

24"X36" 100lb Gloss Book with Aqueous Coating Color Front, No Back.

100	$800.00	$8.00 each
250	$1,500.00	$6.00 each
500	$2,500.00	$5.00 each
1,000	$3,000.00	$3.00 each
2,500	$4,000.00	$1.60 each
5,000	$6,000.00	$1.20 each
10,000	$8,000.00	$0.80 each

24"X38" 100lb Gloss Book with Aqueous Coating Color Front, No Back.

100	$900.00	$9.00 each
250	$1,750.05	$7.00 each
500	$3,000.00	$6.00 each
1,000	$3,800.00	$3.80 each
2,500	$4,500.00	$1.80 each
5,000	$6,000.00	$1.20 each
10,000	$8,000.00	$0.80 each

26"X39" 100lb Gloss Book with Aqueous Coating Color Front, No Back.

100	$1,000.00	$10.00 each
250	$1,800.00	$7.20 each
500	$2,500.00	$5.00 each
1,000	$3,000.00	$3.00 each
2,500	$5,000.00	$2.00 each
5,000	$7,500.00	$1.50 each
10,000	$8,500.00	$0.85 each

27"X39" 100lb Gloss Book with Aqueous Coating Color Front, No Back.

100	$1,000.00	$10.00 each
250	$1,800.00	$7.20 each
500	$2,500.00	$5.00 each
1,000	$3,000.00	$3.00 each
2,500	$5,000.00	$2.00 each
5,000	$7,500.00	$1.50 each
10,000	$8,500.00	$0.85 each

Postcards

Our standard Postcard is a **4"X6"** 14pt Gloss Coated Cover with UV laminate protection. Color front, B&W Back.

100	$75.00	$0.75 each
250	$150.00	$0.60 each
500	$250.00	$0.50 each
1,000	$300.00	$0.30 each
2,500	$500.00	$0.20 each
5,000	$550.00	$0.11 each
10,000	$600.00	$0.06 each

Rack Cards

Our 14pt. Gloss UV Laminate coated Rack Cards are of the highest quality. Available size is 4"x 9"

Color Front, No Back / Color Front, Black & White Back / Color Both Sides

100	$75.00	$0.75 each
250	$175.00	$0.70 each
500	$300.00	$0.60 each
1000	$500.00	$0.50 each
2500	$1000.00	$0.40 each
5000	$1500.00	$0.30 each
10000	$2000.00	$0.20 each

HINT! As you travel, make sure you hit up every *REST AREA* you pass and put some of your Rack Cards in their display!

Table Tent

Our Table tents are delivered unfolded, printed on 100lb Gloss Cover with Aqueous Coating. You're sure to look great sitting on any table.

4.25x12 folded to 4.25x6

250	$200.00	$0.80 each
500	$325.00	$0.65 each
1000	$500.00	$0.50 each
2500	$750.00	$0.30 each
5000	$1250.00	$0.25 each
10000	$2000.00	$0.20 each

4x12 folded to 4x6

250	$210.00	$0.84 each
500	$375.00	$0.75 each
1000	$600.00	$0.60 each
2500	$1250.00	$0.50 each
5000	$1500.00	$0.30 each
10000	$2000.00	$0.20 each

4x13 folded to 4x6.5

250	$210.00	$0.84 each
500	$375.00	$0.75 each
1000	$600.00	$0.60 each
2500	$1200.00	$0.50 each
5000	$15001500.00	$0.30 each
10000	$2000.00	$0.20 each

4x16 folded to 4x8

250	$275.00	$1.10 each
500	$450.00	$0.90 each
1000	$800.00	$0.80 each
2500	$1500.00	$0.60 each
5000	$2000.00	$0.40 each
10000	$3000.00	$0.30 each

4x8 folded to 4x4

250	$237.50	$0.95 each
500	$375.00	$0.75 each
1000	$600.00	$0.60 each
2500	$1250.00	$0.50 each
5000	$1500.00	$0.30 each
10000	$2000.00	$0.20 each

5x11 folded to 5x5.5

250	$287.50	$1.15 each
500	$500.00	$1.00 each
1000	$800.00	$0.80 each
2500	$1500.00	$0.60 each
5000	$2000.00	$0.40 each
10000	$3000.00	$0.30 each

Yard Signs

Our outdoor Political corrugated Plastic yard signs come with the metal stands included in the price. Our signs are fully printed. We don't cut and apply vinyl letters. We currently offer two sizes 18"x24" or 24"x24" After 5, we sell in multiples of 5.

18"x24" Color Front, No Back

1	$37.00 each
2	$22.50 each
3	$18.33 each
4-9	$17.00 each
10-50	$14.00 each
60-80	$11.00 each
85-95	$10.00 each
100	$ 9.00 each

18"x24" Color Both Sides

1-5	$50.00 each
10-20	$30.00 each
30-50	$18.00 each
60-90	$15.00 each
100	$12.00 each

24"x24" Color Front, No Back

1-5	$37.00 each
10-20	$15.00 each
30-50	$14.00 each
60-90	$12.00 each
100	$10.00 each

24"x24" Color Both Sides

1-5	$50.00 each
10-20	$30.00 each
30-50	$18.00 each
60-90	$15.00 each
100	$12.00 each

CD Duplication

If you already have your audio file completed, anything from music, Preaching Sermons, Teaching Sessions, or Audio books, we can burn your audio onto high quality CD's with an awesome gloss finished print on your CD. These prices do not include any kind of Packaging. They will be delivered on a spindle.

CD's in Bulk

50	$200.00	$4.00 each
100	$300.00	$3.00 each
300	$825.00	$2.75 each
500	$1125.00	$2.25 each
1000	$1750.00	$1.75 each
1500	$1875.00	$1.25 each
2000	$2000.00	$1.00 each
2500	$2375.00	$0.95 each
5000	$3000.00	$0.60 each

Additional Packaging Options Include

Paper CD Sleeve	$0.10 each
Jewel Case Slim	$0.50 each – Does not include artwork design
DVD Case	$0.50 each – Does not include artwork design

Static Window Clings

Because we offer so many sizes and options, please contact us for a custom quote.

Stickers

Because we offer so many sizes and options, please contact us for a custom quote.

Greeting Cards

Because we offer so many sizes and options, please contact us for a custom quote.

Professional Video Commercials for Internet use

We can take your text, video clips, audio and pictures, and produce a high quality video that you can use on all your printed promotional products via the use of a QR code. You can use the video for internet use, or however you choose. The cost is based on 30 second increments. If you provide all the content we need for the video, then you can get your video created for only $50.00.

30 seconds $50.00
60 seconds $100.00

Need an Add On?
An Add-On is music, video files of actors or backgrounds. An Add-On could also be a voiceover.

Copyright Free Music file: $25.00 per file. Not 30 seconds
Studio Produced Music File: $100.00 per file. Not 30 seconds

Copyright Free Video file with actors or movement: $25.00 each. Not based on 30 Seconds. These clips vary in length.
Voiceover male or female: $25.00 per 30 seconds

Film on location: If you need us to come and record you or someone on video, we can do that as well. The cost is $100.00 per hour with a minimum of 1 hour.

Can Koozies - Blank
Quality 4mm Collapsible Soda Can Koozies 1 Color no print.

50	$60.00	$1.20 ea
100	$85.00	$0.85 ea
250	$162.50	$0.65 ea
500	$250.00	$0.50 ea
1000	$499.00	$0.49 ea
2500	$750.00	$0.30 ea

Can Koozies - 1 color & 1 Print color

Quality 4mm Collapsible Can Koozies 1 color. Koozie with 1 color ink print. We have many koozie colors and ink colors, so just let us know what you need.

50	$93.00	$1.86 ea
100	$100.00	$1.00 ea
250	$212.50	$0.85 ea
500	$275.00	$0.55 ea
1000	$500.00	$0.50 ea
2500	$875.00	$0.35 ea

Can Koozies – Full Color

50	$200.00	$4.00 ea
100	$250.00	$2.50 ea
250	$500.00	$2.00 ea
500	$860.00	$1.72 ea
1000	$1500.00	$1.50 ea
2500	$3250.00	$1.30 ea

If you need printing on both sides, please call our office for a custom quote.

Coffee Mugs

Our standard mug is an 11 oz. ceramic mug. The finish is gloss interior and exterior.

12	$144.00	$12.00 ea
24	$240.00	$10.00 ea
36	$252.00	$7.00 ea
72	$360.00	$3.60 ea

Publishing Options without Distribution

Print Runs on Paperback Books with No Publisher Representation

WhosoeverPress.com
256-706-3315
Est. 2012

The costs below DO cover your ISBN & Barcode.
You may order an LOC# if desired.
The costs below DO NOT cover the cost of a book cover.
We do have Professional Designers if you need to purchase a cover Design.
Cover Designs run $250.00 for Paperback.
The cost below is the print cost, and DOES NOT cover shipping.
There is a 1 time set up fee of $250.00, but there is no 10% run off charges.
Your file must be submitted in PDF Format. We can convert your file for $50.00 if needed.

Black & White Interior with all the B&W pictures you want. Includes trim sizes: **5.5"X8.5" 6"X9"   5.06"X7.81"   5"X8" 7"X10"   8"X10"   8.5"X11"**

Page 25 - 200

50	$8.00 each
100	$7.50 each
300	$6.75 each
500	$5.00 each
750	$4.50 each
1000	$4.00 each

Need a larger quantity? Call 256-706-3315 for a quote.

We Can Also:

Plastic Coil Binding

Hard Plastic Laminate Full Color Cover Front and Back $5.00
Black &White interior $0.20 per page. 1 piece of paper front and
back is 2 pages.
Full Color Pages $0.30 per page
Available Sizes 5.5"x 8.5" or 8.5"x11"
Quantity Discounts available after 10 copies

Hardback Printing

Our hardback printing is top of the line quality. There is no way
to provide an accurate price example for hardback printing until
we have your exact page count, trim size, and quantity you
desire. For an exact print quote, please call our offices Monday
– Sunday to speak with a qualified print associate.

Stapled Publishing

We can print and staple your documents together to make a
beautiful 5.5"x8.5" booklet.
If needed, Graphic Designer to create your cover, $250.00
Interior Black and White Pages $0.15/page.
Color interior, text only $0.20/page.
Full Color interior with Bleed, Full Color Artwork, $0.40/page

If you desire for your material to be legally copyrighted with the
US government, please mention so on the phone when you call
in your order.

Printing with Publisher Representation

We currently offer one Publishing Package, at a low cost of only $1,500.00. At a rate like this, anyone who believes in themselves enough, can become a Published Author.

While everything you see is what you get, you may also purchase marketing packages, and additional services from Whosoever Press. This will only enhance your publishing experience.
The Package is as follows:

$1,500.00   Turn-around time 6-8 months

50 books upon publication

ISBN number and barcode

Library of Congress number

Books A Million & Barnes and Noble registered

Registered with Ingram Distribution.

Kindle Edition

100 Full Color Posters   8.5 x 11 (Created based on your Cover design)

100 Full color Book Signing Flyers 8.5 x 11 as the Publishing process is complete.

5,000 Business Cards (Created based on your Cover design)

500 Bookmarks (Created based on your Cover design)

Book listed on Amazon.com

Book listed on Whosoever Press website

Custom Web page on WhosoeverPress.com

Books sold through Whosoever Press Distribution outlets

30 – 60 minutes radio interview with Nate Fortner on The Author Minute Internet show.

Free book editing up to 150 pages. Any additional pages, you (the author), are responsible for paying for editing through Whosoever Press @ $1.50 per page.

Cover design help offered by Whosoever Press. We have a Graphic Designer who will make you look great! You will receive a $500.00 Book Cover included in this Package.

Google search engine help to include your tag words and key phrases so that your book will appear higher in the search engine results.

1 copy of Grant Cardone's "The 10 X Rule"

A video trailer will be created for your book. This will be connected to your book through the QR Code on the back of your book, and all promotional products.

Manuscript submitted for possible review to:

Publishers Weekly
Kirkus Reviews
Booklist
Library Journal
School Library Journal
Horn Book Magazine
Choice
New York Times Book Review
Washington Post Book World
USA Today
Wall Street Journal
New York Review of Books
Voice Literary Supplement

While we do submit your manuscript for a review to these reviewers, we cannot guarantee that your manuscript will be reviewed.

Kirkus Reviews- If you decide that you absolutely must have a Kirkus Review, then visit: www.KirkusReviews.com the cost is $425.00 paid to Kirkus Reviews, not WhosoeverPress.com. If you do decide to get a Kirkus Review, then get on it fast, so we can print that review on the back cover of your book! We do suggest that you spend the extra money!

We post on the Whosoever Press Facebook page about your book to our followers.

We Tweet to our followers about your book as well.

Exposure to Hollywood Movie Producers. If we feel your book has potential to become the next hit Christian Film, we will pass your book on to our contacts in the film industry.

As Whosoever Press Owner Nate Fortner is on the board of The Artists Music Guild, you will be exposed to one of the largest and fastest growing organizations for developing Artists in the United States.

Press Release Distribution to Newspaper, Radio, Television, and online.

We very highly suggest that you start finding magazines that are on the same subject as your book. Get the contact information, and send them a copy of your book and ask for a review. We can print these reviews on your promotional material.
You can visit: www.World-Newspapers.com to get a head start.

Published in the Whosoever Press Magazine. (Launching 2016)

We are now offering Hardback Printing. Must submit for a custom quote. Minimum run print 500 copies.

You will receive a detailed royalty report four times a year at the end of each quarter.

We now also offer Coil Binding Printing Full Color or Black and white. Great for Church Directories, or small studies.

Marketing Packages

Package 1

STANDARD SIZE POSTCARDS / One-Time Mailing

Marketing Consultation- This is where you decide who you want to target.

1,000 Mailing List of target customers (data by InfoUSA)

Design Service

1,000 Quantity – 4" x 6" POSTCARDS

Full Color Both Sides

14 pt. Gloss Coated Cover (C2S) with Gloss UV Lamination on Front Side (Distributed once with our low-cost Mailing Services)

Mailing Services - Presorted First-Class (3-5 business days)

Price $1200.00

Package 2

STANDARD SIZE POSTCARDS / One-Time Mailing

Marketing Consultation- This is where you decide who you want to target.

2,500 Mailing List of target customers (data by InfoUSA)

Design Service

2,500 Quantity – 4" x 6" POSTCARDS

Full Color Both Sides

14 pt. Gloss Coated Cover (C2S) with Gloss UV Lamination on Front Side
(Distributed once with our low-cost Mailing Services)

Mailing Services - Presorted First-Class (3-5 business days)

Price $1,800.00

Package 3

STANDARD SIZE POSTCARDS / One-Time Mailing

Marketing Consultation- This is where you decide who you want to target.

5,000 Mailing List of target customers (data by InfoUSA)

Design Service

5,000 Quantity – 4" x 6" POSTCARDS

Full Color Both Sides

14 pt. Gloss Coated Cover (C2S) with Gloss UV Lamination on Front Side
(Distributed once with our low-cost Mailing Services)

Mailing Services - Presorted First-Class (3-5 business days)

Price $3,500.00

Package 4

JUMBO SIZE POSTCARDS / One-Time Mailing

Marketing Consultation

1,000 Mailing List of target customers (data by InfoUSA)

Design Service

1,000 Quantity – 5.5" x 8.5" POSTCARDS

Full Color Both Sides

14 pt. Gloss Coated Cover (C2S) with Gloss UV Lamination on Front Side (Distributed once with our low-cost Mailing Services)

Mailing Services - Presorted Standard (10-15 business days)

Price $1,300.00

Package 5

JUMBO SIZE POSTCARDS / One-Time Mailing

Marketing Consultation

2,500 Mailing List of target customers (data by InfoUSA)

Design Service

2,500 Quantity – 5.5" x 8.5" POSTCARDS

Full Color Both Sides

14 pt. Gloss Coated Cover (C2S) with Gloss UV Lamination on Front Side (Distributed once with our low-cost Mailing Services)

Mailing Services - Presorted Standard (10-15 business days)

Price $1,900.00

Package 6

JUMBO SIZE POSTCARDS / One-Time Mailing

Marketing Consultation

5,000 Mailing List of target customers (data by InfoUSA)

Design Service

5,000 Quantity – 5.5" x 8.5" POSTCARDS

Full Color Both Sides

14 pt. Gloss Coated Cover (C2S) with Gloss UV Lamination on Front Side
(Distributed once with our low-cost Mailing Services)

Mailing Services - Presorted Standard (10-15 business days)

Price $3,600.00

Don't see what you need? Give us a call at 256-706-3315

Want more than 1,000 sleeves? We offer discounts!

1,000	$250.00	$0.25 each
3,000	$700.00	$0.23333 each
7,000	$1,400.00	$0.20 each
15,000	$.015 each	

Need Higher Quantities call my office.

We can print on a white or brown sleeve. Artwork size: 2.1" X 3"

We can currently print in Black, red, blue, or green ink.
Note! Red ink will turn pink on white sleeves. – This is great for Valentine's Day Sleeves.

Want to do this in your town? Call my office today to start making money! I'll show you how!

Radio Advertisements

We also sell radio advertisements for **Southern Gospel WZCT AM 1330 out of Scottsboro, AL**.

Radio is a great way to promote your business locally. WZCT provides great rates and services to help your business grow with our station. To take advantage of some really awesome radio advertising rates, give us a call.

Call Nate at: Cell: 256-706-3315
Office: 256-574-1330

Email me: Nate@WhosoeverPress.com

Why advertise with us?

Here's Exactly Why!

We are streaming LIVE 24/7 online around the world at: http://SouthernGospelam1330.com
Your advertisement will also stream on Local Scottsboro TV on Channel 10
You will even get shout outs on our Social Media accounts.

We're here to serve your advertising needs in 2016!

1. **100 Spots**- 30 Second spots for _$300.00_ monthly featuring your business

2. **Trade Line: Trade Line-** Available Monday through Friday during the morning show

Option #1: This would include having your business featured with 3-30 second spots in a 15 minute segment for *$125.00* monthly.

Option #2: Having all 5 days of 15 minute segments with 3 spots will be *$300.00.* This will be guaranteed Monday through Friday with your business featured during our popular morning show.

3. **LIVE REMOTES:** We offer on-site coverage speaking LIVE about the goods and services your business provides as well as 5 spots per day for 30 days to let listens know we are coming. We bring $100.00 hotdogs and buns. You just provide the trimmings. We give away CD's and other goodies from the station. You can provide gifts that day if you wish. The cost is ONLY *$500.00*

4. **Community News:** You sponsor this daily at an open time during the morning, noon or evening. 8:00 am, 12:00 pm, or 4:00 pm Monday through Friday. You receive a 15 second spot with the name of your business, a 30 second spot, and a closing 15 second spot. The news will be read between your spots daily for *$150.00* per month if you choose a one-time spot. If you choose to sponsor all three times, it will be discounted to *$400.00* per month.

5. **Church of the Month:** We draw one church each month for a flower arrangement provided by a florist. You as the sponsor along with the florist will get you mentioned as the Church of the Month sponsor 5 times a day Monday through Friday during drive times for a total of *$175.00* a month.

6. **Church Announcements:** You sponsor the daily Church news Monday through Friday 8:05 am, 12:05 pm, and 4:05 pm. You will receive a 15 second spot opening, a

30 second spot in the middle of the news being read, and a 15 second spot closing at the end. If you choose one time, it will be *$150.00* per month. If you decide to sponsor all three times, your discounted rate would be *$400.00* a month.

7. **Forty Eight Hours of Christmas Music:** Every year, we bring the people of northeast Alabama 48 hours of Christmas Music from 6:00 pm December 23rd until Midnight Christmas Day. We invite you to be a part of it, and as a sponsor, you get at least one 30 spot per hour and 50 name mentions for your business. This is a great price at only *$200.00*

8. **Holiday Greetings:** Say hello for any holiday of the year from your business. The greetings will be 15 second spots and run 3 times a day for six days. 5 days prior, and the day of the holiday. Price: *$125.00* 18 total 15 second spots.

9. **Obituary Sponsor:** As we read the local obituaries throughout the day, your business will be mentioned for *$125.00*/month with a 3 month contract.

Want Your Own Show?

What better way to promote your ministry or business than to give locals the opportunity to hear you on your very own show each week. Having your own weekly show will give you the chance to inform, engage, and collect followers for your ministry or business.

30 minute shows run *$45.00*

Listening Area

202

Gift Ideas

Turn your favorite photo or company logo into a journal.

We will print a 100 page Journal, fully lined front and back, giving you 200 pages for writing. You pick what you want on the full color front cover. The Back cover will include a promotional for Whosoever Press. If you want to provide an image for the back cover instead of the Whosoever Press promo, you can do so for an additional one time charge of $10.00. The interior can also include a favorite Bible verse or quote at the bottom of each page.

1-50	$8.00 each
51-100	$6.00 each
101-200	$5.00 each
201-500	$4.85 each
501-1000	$4.00 each

Check out these great sample ideas below!

Scan Code

Journals Are a Great Gift for Any Occasion!

Here's a Few Example Ideas.

Holidays

New Year's - January 1st

Martin Luther King Jr. Day - January 18th

Ground Hog - Day February 2nd

Valentine's Day - February 14th

President's Day - February 15th

St. Patrick's Day - March 17th

Easter - March 27th

Passover - April 23rd

Arbor Day – April 29th

National Day of Prayer - May 5th

Mother's Day – May 8th

Memorial Day – May 30th

Father's Day – June 19th

Independence Day - July 4th

National Grandparents Day – September 11th

Halloween - October 31st

Thanksgiving November 24th

Christmas Day December 25th

Business

Administrative Professionals Day - April 27th

Take your son or daughter to work - April 28th

Nurse's Week – May 6th through May 12th

Boss's Day - October 17th

Success Isn't Free!
Success Isn't Given!
Success Isn't Even Earned!
It's Made!

P.S. – Success Requires Action!

About The Author

Never in my life, have I had anyone come up and take me by the hand, and show me how to grow a company. I've had some advice givers here and there, but never have I had someone teach me the steps I needed to know to grow a company. I don't have a business degree, nor do I have a million in the bank yet. One thing I do know, is the Hustle! I learned real quickly that real success requires action. If you want anything in this life, you better get committed and never give up!

I grew up broke in the mountains of West Virginia, but we didn't know we were poor. My parents worked hard, and provided for me and my sister. My Grandma Margaret was the link that held our entire family together. Being from West Virginia and living in Alabama for the past 10 years, I'm basically a Hillbilly transplant. It hasn't been easy for me to fit in here. I've always been an outsider looking for my place to belong. Then I realized, I don't need to fit in, I need to conquer and destroy so to speak. I was laughed at and made fun of by countless numbers of people when I wrote my first book *"Teaching Christians To Pray the Bible Way."* At one point, I went through a 10 month depression where I just wanted to die. To this day, I still where a bracelet on my wrist that says *NKJV,* Philippians 4:13, "I can do all things through Christ who strengthens me." Without my faith in God to carry me through the tough times in my life, I probably wouldn't be here now to tell you how I overcame.

I have the privilege of traveling across the country singing my songs to crowds of all sizes. I'm a Country Christian Recording Artist, and it's really cool because my music is played on radio stations nationwide. As an Author and Publisher, I get to travel and speak to groups of authors telling my story, and what I'm doing every day to make sure my books are selling and touching lives. As a business owner, I get to help other authors and businesses by providing services that help them to grow their companies. I love being able to help people. At the end of each day, it's a joy for me knowing that I get to help people. Whether it's through my books, my songs, or through my business, I love being able to touch people's lives!

**Success Isn't Free! Success Isn't Given!
Success Isn't Even Earned, It's Made!**